100 True Soliloquies
for Men

Smith and Kraus *Books for Actors*

MONOLOGUE AUDITION SERIES

The Best Men's / Women's Stage Monologues of 2000
The Best Men's / Women's Stage Monologues of 1999
The Best Men's / Women's Stage Monologues of 1998
The Best Men's / Women's Stage Monologues of 1997
The Best Men's / Women's Stage Monologues of 1996
The Best Men's / Women's Stage Monologues of 1995
The Best Men's / Women's Stage Monologues of 1994
The Best Men's / Women's Stage Monologues of 1993
The Best Men's / Women's Stage Monologues of 1992
The Best Men's / Women's Stage Monologues of 1991
The Best Men's / Women's Stage Monologues of 1990
One Hundred Men's / Women's Stage Monologues from the 1980s
2 Minutes and Under: Character Monologues for Actors Volumes I and II
Monologues from Contemporary Literature: Volume I
Monologues from Classic Plays 468 BC to 1960 AD
100 Great Monologues from the Renaissance Theatre
100 Great Monologues from the Neo-Classical Theatre
100 Great Monologues from the 19th Century Romantic and Realistic Theatres
The Ultimate Audition Series Volume I: 222 Monologues, 2 Minutes & Under
The Ultimate Audition Series Volume II: 222 Monologues, 2 Minutes & Under
   from Literature

YOUNG ACTOR MONOLOGUE SERIES

Cool Characters for Kids: 71 One-Minute Monologues
Great Scenes and Monologues for Children, Volumes I and II
Great Monologues for Young Actors, Volumes I and II
Short Scenes and Monologues for Middle School Actors
Multicultural Monologues for Young Actors
The Ultimate Audition Series for Middle School Actors Vol.I: 111 One-Minute
   Monologues
The Ultimate Audition Series for Teens Vol. I: 111 One-Minute Monologues
The Ultimate Audition Series for Teens Vol.II: 111 One-Minute Monologues
The Ultimate Audition Series for Teens Vol.III: 111 One-Minute Monologues
The Ultimate Audition Series for Teens Vol.IV: 111 One-Minute Monologues
The Ultimate Audition Series for Teens Vol.V: 111 One-Minute Monologues
   from Shakespeare
Wild and Wacky Characters for Kids: 60 One-Minute Monologues

If you require prepublication information about upcoming Smith and Kraus
books, you may receive our semiannual catalogue, free of charge, by sending
your name and address to *Smith and Kraus Catalogue, PO Box 127, Lyme, NH
03768. Or call us at (800) 895-4331; fax (603) 643-6431.*

100 True Soliloquies
for Men

edited by Jennie Wyckoff

MONOLOGUE AUDITION SERIES

A SMITH AND KRAUS BOOK

Published by Smith and Kraus, Inc.
177 Lyme Road, Hanover, NH 03755
www.SmithKraus.com

First Edition: July 2004
10 9 8 7 6 5 4 3 2 1

Cover illustration by Lisa Goldfinger
Cover design by Julia Hill Gignoux

Library of Congress Cataloging-in-Publication Data
100 true soliloquies for men / edited by Jennie Wyckoff. —1st ed.
   p. cm. — (Monologue audition series, ISSN 1067-134X)
Companion vol. to: 100 true soliloquies for women.
ISBN 1-57525-304-6
1. Monologues. 2. Acting—Auditions. I. Title: One hundred true soliloquies for men.
II. Wyckoff, Jennie. III. 100 true soliloquies for women. IV. Series.
PN 2080.A155 2003
808.82'45—dc22
2003044106

NOTE: These monologues are intended to be used for audition and class study; permission is not required to use the material for those purposes. However, if there is a paid performance of any of the monologues included in this book, please refer to the permissions acknowledgment pages 135–143 to locate the source that can grant permission for public performance.

Contents

AFTER THE FALL
Arthur Miller

1960s, New York
Quentin, 40s

Quentin sits in a chair facing the audience. He reaches forward toward the Listener, who if he could be seen, would be sitting just beyond the edge of the stage itself. He waits a moment and then speaks.

QUENTIN. Hello! God, it's good to see you again! I'm fine, I just wanted to say hello, really. Thanks. Actually, I called you on the spur of the moment this morning; I have a bit of a decision to make. You know — you mull around about something for months and all of a sudden there it is and . . . I've quit the firm, didn't I write you about that? Really! I was sure I'd written. Oh, about fourteen months ago; a few weeks after Maggie died. It just got to where I couldn't concentrate on a case any more; I felt I was merely in the service of my own success. Although I do wonder sometimes if I am simply trying to destroy myself. — Well, I have walked away from what passes for an important career. — Not very much, I'm afraid; I still live in the hotel, see a few people, read a good deal, stare out the window. God, I wrote you about *that*, didn't I? Maybe I dream these letters. — Mother died. Oh, it's four, five months ago, now. Yes, quite suddenly; I was in Germany at the time and . . . it's one of the things I wanted to talk to you about. I . . . met a woman there. In fact, she's arriving tonight, for some conference at Columbia . . . she's an archeologist. I'm not sure, you see, if I want to lose her, and yet it's outrageous to think of committing myself again. — Well, yes, but look at my life. A life, after all, is evidence, and I have two divorces in my safe-deposit box.

AH, WILDERNESS!

Eugene O'Neill

1906, Connecticut
Richard, 16

Richard waits for Muriel.

RICHARD. Gosh, that music from the hotel sounds wonderful. Must be nearly nine — I can hear the Town Hall clock strike, it's so still tonight — I'll catch hell when I get back, but it'll be worth it. If only Muriel turns up — Am I sure she wrote nine? Yes, it's nine, all right. Aw, that's silly — no, it isn't either — not when you're really in love — Darn it, I wish she'd show up! — think of something else — that'll make the time pass quicker — Last night? — the Pleasant Beach House — Belle — ah, forget her! — now, when Muriel's coming — that's a fine time to think of — ! But I didn't go upstairs with her — even if she was pretty — Aw, she wasn't pretty — she was just a whore — She was everything dirty — Muriel's a million times prettier, anyway — Muriel and I will go upstairs — when we're married — but that will be *beautiful* — But I oughtn't even to think of that yet — it's not right — I'd never — now — but after we're married — That damned barkeep kicking me — I'll bet you if I hadn't been drunk I'd have given him one good punch in the nose — Aw, you deserved a kick in the pants — making such a darned slob of yourself! You must have been a fine sight when you got home! — having to be put to bed and getting sick! Phaw! Think of something else, can't you? Recite something — See if you remember —

"Nay, let us walk from fire unto fire,

From passionate pain to deadlier delight,

I am too young to live without desire,

Too young art thou to waste this summer night —"

Gee, that's a peach! I'll have to memorize the rest and recite it to Muriel the next time — I wish I could write poetry — about her and me — Gee, it's beautiful tonight — as if it was a special night — for me and Muriel — Gee, I love tonight — I love the sand, and the trees, and the grass, and the water, and the sky, and the moon — It's all in me and I'm in it — God, it's so beautiful! There's nine now — I don't see her — She must have got caught. Gee, I hate to go home and catch hell — without having seen her! Aw, who ever heard of a woman being on time — I ought to know enough about life by this time not to expect — There she comes now — Gosh! "And lo, my love, mine own soul's heart" — Mustn't let her know I'm so tickled — If women are too sure of you, they treat you like slaves. Let her suffer for a change —

ALKÊSTIS

Euripides, translated by Carl R. Mueller

Phêrai, Thessaly, Greece.
Outside the palace of King Admêtos.

Enter APOLLO from the palace with bow and quiver.

APOLLO.
> I am Apollo.
> > A god.
> And I have served in this house of Admêtos
> > > as,
> shall we say,
> > a common everyday slave.
> I have eaten the bitter bread of hard-labor;
> I have tended herds of cattle;
> and I have guarded my master's house
> from all manner of evil and
> > > > destruction
> > > for this length of a year.

> My master, I say,
> Admêtos, son of Pherês,
> a splendid and godly man.

> > > It all began,
> this sojourn of mine in captivity,
> when Zeus with one of his bolts of
> > > > > lightning
> stabbed my son Asklêpios through the chest,
> > > killing him.

His reason?
My son raised men from the dead,
and Zeus, my father, felt threatened.

Well, make no mistake,
I retaliated by killing the Cyclopes, those
one-eyed forgers of Zeus' fire.

Punishment for me?
                    Yes, indeed.
        Exile, you might say,
to the earth,
and menial labor in the house of a mortal —
                                        yes,

        godly being that I am.

But back to my kindly master,
                        Admêtos,
whom, yes, I think of as a friend.

I saved him once,
by trickery, no less,
from the Fates, no less.

He was scheduled, you see,
        for an early death,
but I persuaded them
to allow him to live —
                though not without a price,
                on that they insisted —
but only in the event that someone
offered to die in his place,
        substituting their own corpse
to satisfy the dismal powers below.

He looked far and he looked wide,
Admêtos did,
asked for this extreme,
extravagant gift from everyone whose love
he had any claim on.

And found?
Not a soul.
No one.
Not even his parents,
old as they are, agreed.

Well, I said no one,
but there was, of course, Alkêstis.
Alkêstis, his wife.
The one and only
who was willing to give up her
own life;
willing to resign her days
in the sun's bright
radiance.

And this is the day they set aside;
the day for that sad but fated event.
She's in the house now,
dying, you might say,
or on the verge of it;
tended by her family,
loved ones circling her bed,
propping her with anxious, loving arms.

Actually, I'm on my way out of here.
It isn't the way of gods, you see,
to pollute their divinity with the
sight of death.

And so, I leave this house and its dear
walls I've come so to love.

     Ah, but here comes Death,
faithful chaperon to the world of the dead.
I've never known the old boy to be late,
         and here he is now,
         painfully on time.
Though I must admit, he's been
champing at the bit for this day
since god knows when.
               This day of
dear Alkêstis' death.

AMPHITRYON
Moliere, translated by Richard Wilbur

Ancient Greece
Amphitryon, 40s

Amphitryon decides whether to act on his feelings of hate or to stay quiet.

AMPHITRYON. Oh, but he's dealt my soul a staggering blow,
      And given my poor mind a brutal jar!
      If things are as the rascal says they are,
      Look how my love and honor are brought low!
      Whether to hush things up, or to proclaim
          This outrage, reason, must decide.
      Should I speak out in anger, or should I hide
          This blot upon my house and name?
      But need I *think*, when the wrong is so extreme?
      What matter if I publish or conceal?
          Let bitter hate be all I feel,
          And vengeance be my only theme.

AMPHITRYON
Moliere, translated by Richard Wilbur

Ancient Greece
Amphitryon, 40s

Amphitryon tries to make sense of why she would lie.

AMPHITRYON. I cannot find her brother anywhere;
    My search is vain, my weariness complete.
    What could be harsher than the lot I bear?
    The man I seek eludes me, yet as my feet
        Lead me distracted here and there,
    I meet a throng I have no wish to meet.
    A thousand folk I've scarcely seen before,
    Unwitting pests, extol our deeds of war,
    And madden me with their congratulations.
    Tormented as I am by private cares,
    I suffer under this applause of theirs,
    And their embraces sharpen my impatience.
        Vainly I seek to dodge their dread
        Acclaim, for everywhere I fly,
    Their kindly persecution stops me dead;
    And as they gush at me, and I reply
        With shrugs and noddings of the head,
    I mutter curses at them on the sly.
    Ah, me! How little praise and honor mean,
    And all else that brilliant victory brings,
    When the soul is overcome with grief so keen!
    How gladly one would barter all such things
        If the heart could once more be serene!
        Incessantly, my jealous brain
        Dwells on my dark vicissitudes,
        And yet, the more it mulls and broods,
    The less it can untangle or explain.

The theft of the diamonds I can understand;
A seal will not deter a clever thief;
But her claim that they were given her by my hand,
Last night, is baffling and beyond belief.
Twixt men, there can be similarities
Whereby imposters manage to deceive;
But that some crafty rascal could with ease
Impersonate a husband, I can't conceive;
There'd be innumerable disparities
Which any wife would readily perceive.

     As for Thessalian sorcery,
Those famous tales that everybody tells
Of ladies fair seduced through magic spells
Have always seemed preposterous to me;
And it would be a jest of Fate if I,
          Returning from the war in glory,
          Must play the butt of such a story,
          And see my honor lost thereby.
I mean to question her again, and see
If what she said was not a fantasy
Caused by some transient fever of the brain.
     Just Heaven! For my peace of mind,
     Let that be proven; let me find
That she was temporarily insane!

ANDROMACHE

Jean Racine, translated by Richard Wilbur

Ancient Greece
Orestes, 20s – 30s

Orestes discusses his plans with us.

ORESTES. Yes, yes, you'll follow me; the king will give
      His prompt consent; of that I'm positive.
      Pyrrhus will not detain her, never fear:
      He has no eyes but for his Trojan dear.
      All other women weary him; he'll snatch
      At any chance to annul the wedding-match.
      I need but broach the matter. And then, what bliss
      To rob Epirus of a prize like this!
      Keep all that's left of Hector's Troy; protect
      Sons, widows by the thousand; I shan't object,
      Epirus, if Hermione can but sever
      Her fortunes from your Lord, and you, forever.
      But here, but chance, he comes. I'll speak with him.
      To all her charms, Love, let his eyes be dim.

ANNE OF THE THOUSAND DAYS

Maxwell Anderson

1536, England
Henry, 50s

Henry struggles to sign Anne's death warrant.

HENRY. This is hard to do
      when you come to put pen to paper.
      You say to yourself:
      She must die. And she must —
      if things are to go as planned.
      Yes, if they are to go at all.
      If I am to rule
      and keep my sanity and hold my England off the rocks.
      It's a lee shore — and a low tide — and the wind's a gale —
      and the Spanish rocks are bare and sharp.
      Go back to it, Henry, go back to it.
      Keep your mind
      on this parchment you must sign.
      Dip the pen in the ink; write your name.

      You've condemned men, nobles and peasants.
      She's struck down a few herself —
      or driven you to it.
      It's only that a woman you've held in your arms
      and longed for when she was away,
      and suffered with her — no, but she promised you an heir.
            Write it down —
      Write Henry rex, and it's done.
      And then the headsman
      will cry out suddenly, "Look, look there!"
      and point to the first flash of sunrise,
      and she'll look,

not knowing what he means, and his sword will flash
in the flick of the sun, through the little bones of her neck
as she looks away,
and it will be done.
It will be done.

How did I come to this?
What were you like, Henry,
when she flashed her first anger at you
ten years ago in Spring?
How hopeful were you,
how mistaken, then,
how ridiculous,
how much in love?

ANNE OF THE THOUSAND DAYS
Maxwell Anderson

1536, England
Henry, 50s

Even though his hands are steady, Henry can't escape his true feelings about Anne's execution.

HENRY. I've worked all night.
> There's a light in the window.
> They say you need less sleep as you grow older.
> Or more.
> One or the other. This night I've had none.
> *(Puts out a hand.)*
> Yet my hand's steady as a tree.
> And the writing's firm as a boy's.
> This is the morning she's to die. I'd almost forgotten.
> That would have shaken me, ten years ago.
> Not now.
> I need a new pen.
> *(The boom of a single cannon is heard.)*
> Nan is dead. Well, so much for Nan. That's over.
> And so your hands are steady, are they?
> Open the bag you lug behind you, Henry.
> Put in Nan's head.
> Nan's head.
> And her eyes, and the lips you kissed.
> Wherever you go they'll follow after you now.
> Her perfume will linger
> in every room you enter, and the stench
> of her death will drive it out.
> Get on with your work.
> These are not empty things you do.

ART
Yazmina Reza

Present, A City
Marc, 50s – 60s

Marc regrets his aggressive behaviour toward his best friend.

MARC. Obviously I should have taken the Ignatia.

Why do I have to be so categorical?

What possible difference can it make to me, if Serge lets himself be taken in by modern Art?

I mean, it is a serious matter. But I could have found some other way to put it to him.

I could have used a less aggressive tone.

Even if it makes me physically ill that my best friend has bought a white painting, all the same I ought to avoid attacking him about it.

I have to be nicer to him.

From now on, I'm on my best behaviour.

ART

Yazmina Reza

Present, A City
Serge, 50s – 60s

Serge defends his painting.

SERGE. As far as I'm concerned, it's not white.

When I say as far as I'm concerned, I mean objectively. Objectively speaking, it's not white.

It has a white background, with a whole range of greys . . . There's even some red in it.

You could say it's very pale.

I wouldn't like it if it was white. Marc thinks it's white . . . that's his limit . . .

Marc thinks it's white because he's gotten hung up on the idea that it's white.

Unlike Yvan. Yvan can see it isn't white.

Marc can think what he likes, what do I care?

ART
Yazmina Reza

Present, A City
Marc, 50s – 60s

Marc tries to make sense of the fact that his friend has just spent two grand on a piece of junk.

MARC. It's a complete mystery to me, Serge buying this painting. It's unsettled me, it's filled me with some indefinable unease. When I left his place, I had to take three pellets of Gelsemium 9C which Paula recommended — Gelsemium or Ignatia, she said, Gelsemium or Ignatia, which do you prefer, I mean, how the hell should I know? — because I couldn't begin to understand how Serge, my friend, could have bought that picture.

Two hundred thousand francs!

He's comfortable, but he's not rolling in money.

Comfortable, that's all, just comfortable. And he spends two hundred grand on a white painting.

I have to go see Yvan, he's a friend of ours, I have to discuss this with Yvan. Although Yvan's a very tolerant guy, which of course, when it comes to relationships, is the worst thing you can be. Yvan's tolerant because he couldn't care less.

If Yvan tolerates the fact that Serge has spent two hundred grand on some piece of white shit, it means he couldn't care less about Serge. Obviously.

AVOW
Bill C. Davis

Present, American City
Father Raymond, 40s

Father Raymond makes a few announcements.

FR. RAYMOND. Just a few announcements this morning. Members of the Cherished Life Circle will be meeting in the Parish Hall this Wednesday at seven-thirty. Those interested in helping with the annual food drive, please see Valerie Donahue in the vestibule immediately after Mass. *(Pause.)* Also — I'm announcing for the third time, the banns of matrimony between Peter Mullen and Barbara Gorman. For the second, between Arnold Cooper and Tina Hager. Also for the second time, between Herbert Eastwood and Andrea Cipriani. *(Pause.)* And for the first time, I'm announcing the banns of matrimony between Brian Lacey and Thomas Ahearn. Let us pray.

BAKKHAI

Euripides, translated by Carl R. Mueller

Morning, Thebes, Greece.
Before the Royal Palace.

Enter DIONYSOS.

DIONYSOS.
>I am here.
>> I.
>
>Dionysos.
>Fire-born son of Zeus.
>Here in Thebes.
>> I,
>
>once born of Semelê,
>daughter of Kadmos,
>in a blinding burst of lightning.
>>> I, a god
>
>who have hidden my godhead
>and assumed for now
>> human form,
>> disguised as my own
>>>> priest.

>I stand here at the source of the
>> River Dirkê
>> and the waters of Ismênos,
>and I behold, here,
>> by the palace,
>the tomb of my mother,
>> thunderstruck,
>and the ruins of her
>> house, smoking still with the
>> flame of Zeus's fire;

eternal testament
to Hera's savage

           jealousy.

Praise to Kadmos for creating this precinct
      sacrosanct to his daughter's
                honor.
I, in turn,
     have covered it over
with the fresh grape-heavy green of the vine.

THE BOYS NEXT DOOR
Tom Griffin

Present, New England
Arnold, 40s

Arnold introduces himself to us.

ARNOLD. My name is Arnold Wiggins. I'm basically a nervous person. People call me Arnold because I don't have a nickname. So I pretend that Arnold is my nickname so that when people call me Arnold, I pretend that they are close personal friends who know me by my nickname: Arnold. I live here at the Stonehenge Villa apartment complex in a group apartment with three other guys. Did I mention I'm a nervous person? Well, frankly, I am. Today I went to the market at the end of the street to get some Wheaties. But I couldn't remember whether I wanted one box or more boxes, so I asked the manager how many boxes I should get. "For just you?" he said. "Yes, sir," I said. "Seventeen," he said. "Thank you," I said. But, and this is what I want to emphasize by nervous, I could only find nine boxes. So what could I do? *(Pause.)* I got nine boxes of Wheaties. And seven heads of lettuce. That made sixteen. And one bag of charcoal briquets. That made seventeen. And a quart of milk. You know, for the Wheaties. But the more I thought about it, the more I thought I didn't get enough . . . what? Was it (A) lettuce? (B) Wheaties? (C) charcoal briquets? This concerned me. So I asked a girl in line what she thought. I forget what she said, but it was pretty thorough. And then I came home. *(Pause.)* Do you think I did the right thing?

THE BOYS NEXT DOOR
Tom Griffin

Present, New England
Jack, 40s

Jack tells us about the men.

JACK. If Norman joins the army, and Arnold moves to Russia, and Barry goes on the Pro Tour, and Lucien gives his life to agriculture, I'll have a lot more free time. *(A moment.)* Lucien and Norman are retarded. Arnold is marginal. A depressive by trade, he will fool you sometimes, but his deck has no face cards. Barry, on the other hand, really doesn't belong here in the first place. He's a grade A schizophrenic with a chronic history of institutions. Loony, teetering on the edge, but clearly resourceful, Barry tells all his problems to Mrs. Fremus, the deaf widow three apartments down. She knits. He talks. I call it Madame DeFarge and The Golf Pro.

THE BOYS NEXT DOOR
Tom Griffin

Present, New England
Jack, 40s

Here, Jack tells us about his job.

JACK. Sometimes, I eat lunch down here by the railroad tracks. It's very romantic in a sordid kind of way. *(Pause.)* I ran into my ex-wife the other day. She's full of ex-whatever venom. She asked me a few polite questions about my job, then she said, "What happens when they don't need you anymore?" "They'll never not need me anymore," I told her. "Me or somebody else." "Who made that rule?" she asked. "God," I said. *(Pause.)* Three months ago, Lucien was informed by the Social Security Administration that his benefits were being cut off. They said that their information indicated that Lucien was capable of being fully integrated into the community. We appealed. No luck. Our next step is to appear before a State Senate subcommittee. Lucien has been invited as a witness. I try to prepare him, but I don't think it's taking. He says if he knows "The Alphabet Song," it'll be okay. He says he wants to wear a tie with Spiderman on it. Just so they'll know how important this is. *(Pause.)* And as a final note, my ex-wife looked terrific. She drives a BMW now and wears a lot of bright green. "Who's that funny little man in the back seat of your car?" she asked me. It was Arnold. "That's Arnold," I said. "Why is he reading the phone book sideways?" she said. "He's looking for the road map to Russia," I said. "How can you stand it?" she said. And Arnold, still in the back seat of the car, said, "If the phone people don't want to print maps of Russia, fine. But don't turn around and call it a phone book. Don't deceive the public."

THE BUNGLER

Moliere, translated by Richard Wilbur

1600s, Sicily
Mascarille, 30s – 40s

Mascarille tries to convince himself that honor is the best route, not revenge.

MASCARILLE. Hush, my good nature; you haven't a grain of sense,
     And I'll no longer hear your arguments.
     It's you, my anger, that I'll listen to.
     Am I obliged forever to undo
     The blunders of a clod? I should resign!
     That fool has spoiled too many schemes of mine.
     And yet, let's think about this matter coolly.
     Were I to let my just impatience rule me,
     They'd say that I'd been quick to call it quits,
     And that I'd lost the vigor of my wits;
     And what then would become of my renown
     As the most glorious trickster in the town,
     A reputation that I've earned by never
     Failing to think of something wildly clever?
     O Mascarille, let honor be your guide!
     Persist in those great works which are your pride,
     And though your master irks you, persevere
     Not for his sake, but for your own career.
     Yet what can you accomplish, when the force
     Of a demonic head wind blocks your course,
     And you're compelled to tack and tack again?
     What is the use of persevering, when
     His folly brings continual heavy weather,
     And sinks the best schemes you can put together?
     Well, out of kindness, let us give it one
     Final attempt, and see what can be done;
     Then, if he wrecks our chances as before,

I swear that I'll not help him anymore.
We might, in fact, accomplish our desire
If we could get our rival to retire —
If, backing off, Leandre would allow
Me one whole day for the plot I'm hatching now.
Yes, I'm now thinking out an artful plan
Which surely will succeed, if I but can
Remove the obstacle I've spoken of.
He's coming: I'll test the firmness of his love.

THE CHOSEN
Aaron Posner and Chaim Potok

1940s, Brooklyn
Reuven, 30s

Reuven walks through his old home again in his memory.

REUVEN. As I rode home from the hospital with my father that June afternoon, and I put on my spare glasses, the world suddenly seemed to
leap into focus. Everything looked fresh and clean and new. And as I
walked through our house I felt as though I were actually *seeing* it for the
first time. The worn gray carpet and the pictures of Herzl and Chaim
Weizmann in the entrance hall; the smell of chicken soup coming from
the kitchen; my bed; my desk; my books; the war maps; and the pictures
of President Roosevelt and Albert Einstein that I had cut out of *Senior
Scholastic* and pasted on my walls; even the ailanthus tree just outside my
window, everything . . . Everything seemed sharpened, and pulsing with
life. I remember feeling that I had somehow crossed into another world,
as if a little piece of my old self lay shattered in the school yard along with
my glasses.

THE CIDER HOUSE RULES, PART ONE
Peter Parnell

1920s, Maine
Homer, 20s – 30s

Homer talks about what happened to the baby.

HOMER. It would have been a boy. That much is clear. *(He writes in a notebook.)* A woman stabbed when the pregnancy was nearly full-term. The child — rather, the fetus, at nearly nine months, hadn't escaped one of the stab wounds. Source of bleeding . . . source of bleeding . . . *(Homer takes scissors and starts to cut.)* Opening the fetus' sternum. Cutting straight up the middle, noticing immediately the slashed pulmonary artery. Wound is — gosh, only half an inch or so away from an open ductus . . . such a huge ductus arteriosus, half the size of the aorta . . . Can that be? . . . Never looked inside a fetus before. In the BORN, within ten days, the ductus becomes nothing but a fibrous thread. That's because the first baby's breath closes the ductus and opens the lungs. In the fetus, the ductus is a shunt, the blood bypassing the lungs on the way to the aorta. Because a fetus doesn't breathe. And yet so big, the ductus so big . . . because this little fetus never got a chance to breathe . . . to take its first breath . . . *(Pause.)* What, after all, is the life of an embryo but a history of development? *(He turns to look at pictures from* Gray's Anatomy.*)* If we look at *Gray's Anatomy* . . . The head, estimated at twenty-seven days old — not quick, and not recognizably human, either. Barely a spine, no spine, really, just something cocked, like a wrist, and where the knuckles of the fist would be, the ill-formed face of a fish. The undersurface of the head gapes like an eel. But then, in eight weeks, though still not quick, the embryo has a nose and mouth . . . and an expression . . . *(Pause. He stares at the fetus.)* An expression . . . is that . . . ? *(He starts to clean it. He takes it to the sink and washes it.)* There's a spot of old blood on the tray. *(He looks at the fetus.)* Is that . . . an expression . . . ? And for the first time, he saw . . .

Here are elbows, forearms, chest, cheeks, good God, the tiny fingers of its hands . . . A little caked blood on its penis . . . It's tiny . . . little . . . penis . . . *(Pause.)* An expression . . . Is that . . . a smile . . . ? Is it . . . smiling . . . ?

CONVERSATIONS AFTER A BURIAL

Yazmina Reza

Present, France
Alex, 40s

Alex talks to his dead father.

ALEX. Listen, Dad. You don't have much choice but to listen, what with your nostrils full of earth, no more shouting, eh? Now it's me, shouting on my own, shouting non-stop. When I look at myself, I feel like a little old man. I'm shouting, snapping away like a lap-dog, there's something pinched, here, around my mouth. When I was twelve, you slapped me once, because I was eating a chicken leg with one hand. No warning, you didn't even say, 'Use two hands,' you slapped me without a word of warning. Nobody moved a muscle. I went up to my room, sobbing like an idiot. Nathan came up — once he'd finished eating — and said 'He's like that because Mummy died,' my answer was: 'Fuck off, all he has to do is die himself . . .'

CYCLOPS

Euripides, translated by Carl R. Mueller

Sicily.
At the foot of Mt. Aitna.
Outside the cave of Polyphêmos.
Silênos, 50s – 60s

Enter SILÊNOS from the cave, grumbling and carrying a rake.

SILÊNOS.

　　　　　O Dionysos,
the troubles I've gone through for you,
the pains, the labors —
as many now as when I was

　　　　　　　　　young and fit!
I remember that first time,
the time Hera drove you raving

　　　　　　　out of your mind,
and off you took,
deserting the mountain nymphs, your nannies,
　　　and I went after you.
And then the war with the Giants,
　　　that earthborn brood,
　　　and I never left your side,
flank to flank all the way,
me on the right,
covering you with a spear in one hand,
　　　shield in the other.
And I struck that ugly mountain of a
　　　　　　　Giant Enkelados
right through the button of his shield,
and guts all over the place!

— Hm. Did I or didn't I?
Am I dreaming all this?
Have I begun to believe my own tales?
No, by Zeus, I even showed my
        war-spoils to Dionysos himself!
But not all those labors
can hold a candle to the trouble I'm in now.
        You remember, master,
when Hera sicked that band of Tuscan
                pirates on you,
and they set out to sell you into slavery
                in a foreign land?
Well, when I got wind of that,
I and my satyr sons set sail in a second.
There I stood at the stern,
steering the double-oared ship,
while my boys heaved at the oars
                either side,
    plowing the gray sea white with their effort,
and all in search of you, lord.

        Ah,
but then as we rounded Cape Malea,
a monster east wind knocked us off-course
and straight into this craggy land
        near the foot of Aitna.
And we know what that means, don't we?

        Cyclopes!
    Sons of Poseidon!

It's where they live,
        in caves far off the beaten track.
One-eyed monsters with a preference
                for men —

31

they eat them raw.
And one of this brood caught us,
    satyr sons and all,
and keeps us now as slaves in his house.

Polyphêmos he calls himself;
    and he's our master now.
So instead of the dancing reels of
              Dionysos,
we now herd this godless Cyclops' flocks.
And because my satyr sons are young,
they're shepherding young sheep on
            far-off hillsides.

OIMOI!

        As for me,
my duties take a more domestic turn.
I fill up his troughs,
    I sweep out his cave,
and I play chef for this Cyclops' disgusting meals.
Which reminds me —
        duty is duty —
and that cave needs sweeping of a lot more
than dust before the master returns with his —
sheep and goats.

DANCING AT LUGHNASA
Brian Friel

1930s, Ireland
Michael, 20s

Michael tells us about his Uncle Jack.

MICHAEL. When I saw Uncle Jack for the first time the reason I was so shocked by his appearance was that I expected — well, I suppose, the hero from a schoolboy's book. Once I had seen a photograph of him radiant and splendid in his officer's uniform. It had fallen out of Aunt Kate's prayer book and she snatched it from me before I could study it in detail. It was a picture taken in 1917 when he was a chaplain to the British forces in East Africa and he looked — magnificent. But Aunt Kate had been involved locally in the War of Independence; so Father Jack's brief career in the British army was never referred to in that house. All the same the wonderful Father Jack of that photo was the image of him that lodged in my mind.

But if he was a hero to me, he was a hero and a saint to my mother and to my aunts. They pored over his occasional letters. They prayed every night for him and for his lepers and for the success of his mission. They scraped and saved for him — sixpence here, a shilling there — sacrifices they made willingly, joyously, so that they would have a little money to send to him at Christmas and for his birthday. And every so often when a story would appear in the *Donegal Enquirer* about 'our own leper priest,' as they called him — because Ballybeg was proud of him, the whole of Donegal was proud of him — it was only natural that our family would enjoy a small share of that fame — it gave us that little bit of status in the eyes of the parish. And it must have helped my aunts to bear the shame Mother brought on the household by having me — as it was called then — out of wedlock.

THE DEATH OF BESSIE SMITH
Edward Albee

1930s, Tennessee
Jack, 40s

Jack enters, addresses his remarks offstage and to an invisible mirror.

JACK. Hey . . . Bessie! C'mon, now. Hey . . . honey? Get your butt out
of bed . . . wake up. C'mon; the goddam afternoon's half gone; we gotta
get movin'. Hey . . . I called that son-of-a-bitch in New York . . . *I* told
him, all right. I told him what you said. Wake up, baby, we gotta get out
of this dump; I gotta get you to Memphis 'fore seven o'clock . . . and
then . . . POW! . . . *we* are headin' straight north. Here we come; NEW
YORK. I told that bastard . . . I said: Look, you don't have no exclusive
rights on Bessie . . . nobody's got 'em . . . Bessie is doin' you a favor . . .
she doin' you a goddam favor. She don't *have* to sing for you. I said:
Bessie's tired . . . she don't wanna travel now. An' he said: You don't
wanna back out of this . . . Bessie told me *herself* . . . and I said: Look . . .
don't worry yourself . . . Bessie said she'd cut more sides for you . . . she
will . . . she'll make all the goddam new records you want. . . . What
I mean to say *is*, just don't you get any ideas about havin' exclusive
rights . . . because nobody's got 'em. I told him you was free as a bird,
honey. Free as a goddam bird. Some bird! I been downstairs to check us
out. I go downstairs to check us out, and I run into a friend of mine . . .
and we sit in the bar and have a few, and he says: What're *you* doin' now;
what're you doin' in this crummy hotel? And I say: I am cartin' a bird
around with me. I'm cartin' her north; I got a fat lady upstairs; she is
sleepin' off last night. An' he says: You always got *some* fat lady upstairs,
somewhere; boy, I never seen it fail. An' I say: This ain't just no plain fat
lady I got upstairs . . . this is a celebrity, boy . . . this is a rich old fat
singin' lady . . . an' he laughed an' he said: Boy, who you got up there? I
say: You guess. An' he says: C'mon . . . I can't guess. An' I told him . . . I
am travelin' with Miss Bessie Smith.

DEFYING GRAVITY

Jane Anderson

1980s, Florida
C.B., any age

C.B. reads us a letter and explains the situation.

C.B. *(Reading.)* Dear Elizabeth, I'm writing to you on behalf of the men who worked on the ground crew of shuttle flight 51-L. We want you to know how much all of us admired your mother and we offer our sincerest condolences to you and your family. *(He puts the letter down.)* I volunteered to write this letter because I feel partly responsible for what happened. I don't know what you remember, but there were a lot of false starts before your mom's ship finally got off the ground. Some of the delays had to do with the weather, but one of the delays had to do with human error. This human error delay took place on a day that would've been perfect for a lift off. The weather was clear and the sky was a beautiful bright blue. It was as if God just lifted up a giant man-hole cover and said aim here. Well, at T minus nine minutes they couldn't get the handle off of one of the hatches and they had to get this special drill. But when that arrived it didn't work because someone used it and didn't bother to replace the batteries. Let me just explain the situation. See, I borrowed the drill to fix the door on my van. So after work I used the drill then stuck a note on it saying to change the batteries. But I used a post-it that I took off someone's door and the sticky stuff on the back was kinda used up and I guess it didn't stay on the drill. I should've just changed the batteries myself but in order to do that I would've had to fill out a form explaining why I needed the new batteries and then I'd have to run it over to another building to get it approved, then wait an hour to have it processed then run to another building to pick the batteries up, then I would of had to get a guy to supervise me while I put the batteries in, and hell I was at the end of a twenty hour shift of regulating a bunch of LOX bleed valves and my next shift was in five hours. So instead

I went to a local place to wind down. It's a place where a lot of us hung out with your mom and the other astronauts. Once, I played her a game of darts. She beat the heck out of me. You would have been proud. She also won the football pool. What I'm trying to say here is that we saw your mom every day. The last thing any of us wanted to do was to send her up in a ship that was gonna fall apart. I'm sorry. I'm so sorry. I never meant to take your mommy away from you. *(going back to letter)* She was a great example to us all and will live long in our memories as a pioneer of our times. We extend our best wishes for your future and hope that as your mother did, you will be able to follow your dreams. Sincerely Yours, C.B. Williams and the men of Ground Crew number 7749, Division Eighty-six, Department K699-99, Kennedy Space Center.

DEFYING GRAVITY

Jane Anderson

1980s, Florida
Monet, any age

Monet tells us a story about his work.

MONET. During an exhibition of my work, I watched a woman scrutinize one of my paintings. She had her face so close to the canvas, I was afraid that she would come away with paint fixed to the end of her nose. I heard her say to her companion, I'm sorry, but there are too many colors here. I have no idea what I'm looking at. I said to her, if you step back, Madame, perhaps you'll have a better view. She did as I suggested. Oh, is it a building? Yes, it's the Cathedral of Rouen. I live in Rouen, she said, but this isn't what it looks like. This is the cathedral at dawn, I said, perhaps you were still in bed. She went to the next painting. And what is this? That is the cathedral at ten in the morning. I don't see it, she said. She went to the next. And what about this? That is the cathedral at noon. No, I still don't see it. I was about to tell the woman that she had about as much perception as a slug, when she stopped in front of a painting of the cathedral at dusk. She stared at it for a moment then said, yes I recognize it now. You must be a very late sleeper, I said. And she looked at me with a terrible sadness in her eyes, No, Monsieur, this is the time of day when I go to light a candle for my husband. I lived long enough to see the invention of the airplane, but I never went up in one. At that time only the very brave and the very stupid were willing to fly. I once made arrangements to go up in a hot air balloon, but the fog kept us in, which was just as well because the pilot was drunk. I never saw the earth from anything higher than the bell tower of the Cathedral of Rouen. It was a wonderful view. I would have loved to have taken my paints up there, but the priest in charge was a narrow-minded wretch who believed that painters had no right to alter the perfection of God's world. What an idiot. But I always dreamed of seeing the earth from high above. Not just a bird's eye view, but God's view. And when I died, that one last thing I had on my mind.

DEFYING GRAVITY

Jane Anderson

1980s, Florida
Monet, any age

Here, Monet tells us about his process.

MONET. I had to master the conditions of space before I could start to paint. One can't simply throw one's brush down and pick up another as you do on Earth, as anything you put aside will float away. But thanks to a wonderful material called Velcro, I've been able to keep my tubes fastened to my smock. However I do tend to lose track of the caps and must hunt them down like butterflies when I'm done. The paint itself is thick enough so that if I'm careful it will stay adhered to the palette. But sometimes in my enthusiasm I will squeeze a tube too hard and the paint will float away from me in the form of a brightly colored snake. The view outside the window is quite intriguing. There is no horizon line to speak of. Just patterns of clouds and land and sea and a clear, fantastic light. Every ninety minutes we circle the Earth and I have the pleasure of watching sixteen sunsets a day. My only regret is that it passes by so fast. When I painted my series of the cathedral, I used to be enormously frustrated with the rapid change of light, but the time I had then was luxurious compared to what I have now. So I've lined up six canvases in a row and I work on each section of the Earth as we sail by. And when we pass into night I load up my palette with paint so I'm ready to start back on canvas number one. I have fifteen orbits in which to finish my paintings until the Earth shifts into another time of day. I plan to paint every piece of Earth in every kind of light. I'm very much looking forward to seeing the Mediterranean at sunrise and I hear that the French Alps are quite spectacular at dusk. I have been painting for four straight days now. I have no desire to eat or sleep. My body is no longer of consequence. I have only eyes and a hand and a brush and paint and the sun endlessly bouncing colors off the Earth. And I will continue to paint as long as this wonderful rocket will keep me in space.

DON CARLOS

Friedrich von Schiller, translated by Carl R. Mueller

1600s, Spain
King, 40s – 50s

The King asks for help.

KING.

> Great Providence, give me a man!
> I have had much from you, I know,
> but give me now the man I need!
> Bless me with him, great Providence!
> You who are alone,
> you whose eyes see all,
> give me a friend, for my eyes see but little.
> The servants, the helpers you sent me,
> you know, you know what they are to me,
> you know what they are worth,
> and they have been paid what they deserve,
> they whose petty vices, held within bounds,
> have served my ends as your
> tempests serve your ends in ordering creation.
> Great Providence, I need truth now,
> a helper to dig for truth
> where kings are not permitted,
> where their fate does not lead.
> Give me that man of men with an open heart,
> whose clearness of spirit affords him impartial eyes,
> for he will lead me to truth.
> I will shake out the lots of destiny,
> and among those thousands who flutter like moths
> around the imperial flame,
> let me find him,
> let me find that one.

DON CARLOS

Friedrich von Schiller, translated by Carl R. Mueller

Marquis, any age

Excited for this opportunity, the Marquis speaks.

MARQUIS OF POSA.
> A moment rare as this comes only once
> and to lose it is unthinkable.
> Yes, yes,
> this courtier teaches a useful lesson,
> and yet I will not use it as he understands it,
> but as I do.
> How is it that I'm here?
> Is it chance that shows me my reflection in these mirrors?
> Or is it coincidence? Coincidence that
> chooses me from many millions,
> chooses me, the least likely of all.
> What struck the King, what influenced his choice?
> More, I think, than coincidence.
> What is coincidence but rough stone
> brought to life by the sculptor's hand?
> Providence it is that sends coincidence,
> which then we shape to our own ends.
> Whatever it is he wants of me, the King,
> is little concern of mine. And yet,
> what I want of him I know very well.
> If I can but cast the merest spark of truth,
> cast it boldly, into the tyrant's mind,
> how Providence will make it blaze!
> What once appeared so arbitrary,
> so coincidental, may prove in the end
> to have been useful as well as significant.
> Well, if it is, it is, if not, then not.
> I do what I do, because I believe.

DR. FAUSTUS

Christopher Marlowe

1500s, England
Faustus, 30s – 40s

Faustus in his study tries to organize his thoughts.

FAUSTUS. Settle my studies, Faustus, and begin
   To sound the depth of that thou wilt profess;
   Having commenc'd, be a divine in show.
   Yet level at the end of every art,
   And live and die in Aristotle's works.
   Sweet Analytics, 'tis thou hast ravish'd me,
   Bene disserere est finis logices.
   Is to dispute well logic's chiefest end?
   Affords this art no greater miracle?
   Then read no more, thou hast attain'd the end;
   A greater subject fitteth Faustus' wit.
   Summum bonum medicinae sanitas,
   "The end of physic is our body's health."
   Why, Faustus, hast thou not attain'd that end?
   Is not thy common talk sound Aphorisms?
   Are not thy bills hung up as monuments,
   Whereby whole cities have escap'd the plague,
   And thousand desperate maladies been eas'd?
   Yet art thou still but Faustus and a man.
   Wouldst thou make men to live eternally,
   Or, being dead, raise them to life again?
   Then this profession were to be esteem'd.
   Physic, farewell. — Where is Justinian?   *(Reads.)*
   Si una eademque res legatur duobus, alter rem, alter valorem rei.
   A pretty case of paltry legacies!   *(Reads.)*
   Exhaereditare filium non potest pater nisi.
   Such is the subject of the Institute

And universal Body of the Law.
His study fits a mercenary drudge,
Who aims at nothing but external trash;
Too servile and illiberal for me.
When all is done, divinity is best;
Jerome's Bible, Faustus, view it well.   *(Reads.)*
Stipendium peccati mors est. Ha! *Stipendium.*
"*The reward of sin is death.*" That's hard.   *(Reads.)*
Si peccasse negamus, fallimur, et nulla est in nobis veritas.
"If we say that we have no sin we deceive ourselves, and there's
              no truth in us." Why then, belike we must sin and so
              consequently die.
Ay, we must die an everlasting death.
What doctrine call you this, *Che sera sera,*
"What will be shall be?" Divinity, adieu!
These metaphysics of magicians
And necromantic books are heavenly;
Lines, circles, scenes, letters, and characters,
Ay, these are those that Faustus most desires.
O what a world of profit and delight,
Of power, of honour, of omnipotence
Is promis'd to the studious artisan!
All things that move between the quiet poles
Shall be at my command. Emperors and kings
Are but obeyed in their several provinces,
Nor can they raise the wind or rend the clouds;
But his dominion that exceeds in this
Stretcheth as far as doth the mind of man.
A sound magician is a mighty god:
Here, Faustus, try thy brains to gain a deity.

DR. FAUSTUS

Christopher Marlowe

1500s, England
Faustus, 30s – 40s

Faustus shares his thoughts with the audience.

FAUSTUS. Now that the gloomy shadow of the earth
      Longing to view Orion's drizzling look,
      Leaps from th'antarctic world unto the sky,
      And dims the welkin with her pitchy breath,
      Faustus, begin thine incantations,
      And try if devils will obey thy hest,
      Seeing thou hast pray'd and sacrific'd to them.
      Within this circle is Jehovah's name,
      Forward and backward anagrammatis'd,
      The breviated names of the holy saints,
      Figures of every adjunct to the Heavens,
      And characters of signs and erring stars,
      By which the spirits are enforc'd to rise:
      Then fear not, Faustus, but be resolute,
      And try the uttermost magic can perform.

Sint mihi Dei Acherontis propitii! Valeat numen triplex Jehovae! Ignei, aerii, aquatani spiritus, salvete! Orientis princeps Belzebub, inferni ardentis monarcha, et Demogorgon, propitiamus vos, ut appareat et surgat Mephistophilis! Quid tu moraris? Per Jehovam, Gehennam, et consecratum aquam quam nunc spargo, signumque crucis quod nunc facio, et per vota nostra, ipse nunc surgat nobis dicatus Mephistophilis!

THE DUCHESS OF MALFI
John Webster

1500s, Italy
Bosola, any age

Bosola reads us a paper of Antonio's.

BOSOLA. Antonio hereabout did drop a paper —
        Some of your help, false friend — O, here it is:
        What's here? a child's nativity calculated!

(Reads.) The duchess was delivered of a son, 'tween the hours twelve and one, in the night: Anno Dom. 1504, — that's this year *— decimo nono Decembris, —* that's this night *— taken according to the meridian of Malfi —* that's our duchess: happy discovery! *— The lord of the first house, being combust in the ascendant, signifies short life: and Mars being in a human sign, joined to the tail of the Dragon, in the eighth house, doth threaten a violent death, caetera non scrutantur.*

        Why now 'tis most apparent: this precise fellow
        Is the duchess' bawd: — I have it to my wish;
        This is a parcel of intelligency
        Our courtiers were cas'd up for! It needs must follow
        That I must be committed on pretence
        Of poisoning her; which I'll endure, and laugh at: —
        If one could find the father now! but that
        Time will discover. Old Castruchio
        I'th' morning posts to Rome; by him I'll send
        A letter, that shall make her brothers' galls
        O'erflow their livers — this was a thrifty way.
        Though lust do mask in ne'er so strange disguise,
        She's oft found witty, but is never wise.

EDWARD II

Christopher Marlowe

1600s, England
Gaveston, 20s – 30s

Gaveston speaks of his loyalty to the king.

GAVESTON. 'My father is deceased, come Gaveston,
    And share the kingdom with thy dearest friend.'
    Ah, words that make me surfeit with delight!
    What greater bliss can hap to Gaveston
    Than live and be the favourite of a king?
    Sweet prince I come; these, these thy amorous lines
    Might have enforced me to have swum from France,
    And, like Leander, gasped upon the sand,
    So thou wouldst smile and take me in thy arms.
    The sight of London to my exiled eyes
    Is as Elysium to a new-come soul;
    Not that I love the city or the men,
    But that it harbours him I hold so dear,
    The king, upon whose bosom let me die,
    And with the world be still at enmity.
    What need the arctic people love star-light
    To whom the sun shines both by day and night?
    Farewell base stooping to the lordly peers;
    My knee shall bow to none but to the king.
    As for the multitude, that are but sparks
    Raked up in embers of their poverty,
    Tanti! I'll fan first on the wind,
    That glanceth at my lips and flieth away.
    But how now, what are these?

ENTER LAUGHING

Joseph Stein

1930s, New York City
Foreman, middle-aged

Foreman expresses his frustration to the audience and over the phone.

FOREMAN. *(Into phone.)* Hello? . . . Yes, this is Foreman Machines, who you want? . . . Mr. Kolowitz. *Mr.* Kolowitz? You mean David. He ain't here. He's delivering. . . . Call back when he's here. *(Hangs up, abruptly. Talks to himself.)* Mr. Kolowitz! Every peanut in America is a mister; President Roosevelt is a mister, Albert Einstein is a mister and my foolish delivery boy is also a mister — America! *(Phone rings. Shouts at phone on second ring.)* What is it? What? *(Rises, picks up phone.)* Hello? What? I told you he's delivering. I should tell him *who's* calling? Wanda? What kind of name is Wanda? Are you a Jewish girl? . . . All right. I'll tell him when he comes. *(Hangs up, to self.)* Mixed up with girls already. . . . A nothing, fourteen dollars and fifty cents a week, mixed up with girls. . . . She ain't Jewish! . . . Ah, why should I worry; let his father worry. . . . Everything's a *mister! (Shakes head, disbelievingly.)* America!

ENTER LAUGHING
Joseph Stein

1930s, New York City
David, 20s

David makes several phone calls.

DAVID. Hello, Operator, Jerome 8275. *(He waits.)* Hello, Papa? Listen, Papa, I won't be home for supper. No, I'm all right. I'm going to a kind of night school. For acting. Acting . . . like in the movies. . . . No, don't put Mama on. . . . I'll tell you when I . . . Hello, Mama. . . . I'll eat at a restaurant, Mama. . . . Eggs. Okay, meat. . . . No, don't wait up for me, Mama, I'll be home late. . . . Goodbye, Mama. . . . Okay, Ma, sure . . . all right . . . okay . . . all right . . . *(Hangs up.)* Operator, I got the wrong number. I wanted Tremont 8067. . . . Thank you. I trust I haven't kept you waiting too long, but — *(pause)* Hello, Wanda? It's Dave. Listen to this, I went for a job in a play, and they hired me. . . . Yes, as an actor. There were about twelve other fellows, but they hired me. . . . No, I'm not kidding. Listen, I have to eat supper and get back. . . . I don't know, eggs or something. . . . Okay, meat. . . . So long, Wanda. *(Hangs up.)* Hello, Operator, I got the wrong number. . . . I wanted Fordham 7648. Thanks . . . I trust I haven't kept you waiting too long, but in my grief . . . *(then)* Hi, Marvin? David. I did it. No kidding, they picked me from the whole bunch. About twenty guys. . . . And listen, Marv . . . I got a date tonight with the leading lady. Gorgeous. We're going to go over some love scenes, know what I mean? . . . You said it. By the way, Marv, did that laugh sound okay? Just now, when I just laughed — did that sound like a person laughing? Never mind — I'll tell you about it tomorrow. Goodbye.

EQUUS

Peter Shaffer

Present, England
Dysart, 40s

Dysart's inner thoughts are shared with us.

DYSART. With one particular horse, called Nugget, he embraces. The animal digs its sweaty brow into his cheek, and they stand in the dark for an hour — like a necking couple. And of all nonsensical things — I keep thinking about the *horse!* Not the boy: the horse, and what it may be trying to do. I keep seeing that huge head kissing him with its chained mouth. Nudging through the metal some desire absolutely irrelevant to filling its belly or propagating its own kind. What desire could that be? Not to stay a horse any longer? Not to remain reined up for ever in those particular genetic strings? Is it possible, at certain moments we cannot imagine, a horse can add its sufferings together — the nonstop jerks and jabs that are its daily life — and turn them into *grief?* What use is grief to a horse? You see, I'm lost. What use, I should be asking, are questions like these to an overworked Psychiatrist in a provincial hospital? They're worse than useless: they are in fact, subversive. The thing is, I'm desperate. You see, I'm wearing that horse's head myself. That's the feeling. All reined up in old language and old assumption, straining to jump clean-hoofed on to a whole new track of being I only suspect there is. I can't see it, because my educated, average head is being held at the wrong angle. I can't jump because the bit forbids it, and my own basic force — my horsepower, if you like — is too little. The only thing I know for sure is this: a horse's head is finally knowable to me. Yet I handle children's heads — which I must presume to be more complicated, at least in the area of my chief concern . . . In a way, it has nothing to do with this boy. The doubts have been there for years, piling up steadily in this dreary place. It's only the extremity of this case that's made them active. I know that. The *extremity* is the point! All the same, whatever the reason, they are now, these doubts, not just vaguely worrying — but intolerable . . . I'm sorry. I'm not making much sense. Let me start properly: in order. It began one Monday last month with Hesther's visit.

EQUUS
Peter Shaffer

Present, England
Dysart, 40s

Dysart recounts his dream.

DYSART. That night, I had this very explicit dream. In it I'm a chief priest in Homeric Greece. I'm wearing a wide gold mask, all noble and bearded, like the so-called Mask of Agamemnon found at Mycenae. I'm standing by a thick round stone and holding a sharp knife. In fact, I'm officiating at some immensely important ritual sacrifice, on which depends the fate of the crops or of a military expedition. The sacrifice is a herd of children: about five hundred boys and girls. I can see them stretching away in a long queue, right across the plain of Argos. I know it's Argos because of the red soil. On either side of me stand two assistant priests, wearing masks as well: lumpy, pop-eyed masks, such as also were found at Mycenae. They are enormously strong, these other priests, and absolutely tireless. As each child steps forward, they grab it from behind and throw it over the stone. Then, with a surgical skill which amazes even me, I fit in the knife and slice elegantly down to the navel, just like a seamstress following a pattern. I part the flaps, sever the inner tubes, yank them out and throw them hot and steaming on to the floor. The other two then study the pattern they make, as if they were reading hieroglyphics. It's obvious to me that I'm tops as chief priest. It's this unique talent for carving that has got me where I am. The only thing is, unknown to them, I've started to feel distinctly nauseous. And with each victim, it's getting worse. My face is going green behind the mask. Of course, I redouble my efforts to look professional — cutting and snipping for all I'm worth: mainly because I know that if ever those two assistants so much as glimpse my distress — and the implied doubt that this repetitive and smelly work is doing any social good at all — I will be the next across the stone. And then, of course — the damn mask begins to slip. The priests both turn and look at it — it slips some more — they see the green sweat running down my face — their gold pop-eyes suddenly fill up with blood — they tear the knife out of my hand . . . and I wake up.

FAUST: PART ONE

Johann Wolfgang von Goethe,
translated by Carl R. Mueller

1700s, Germany
Faust, 40s

Faust tries to work things out.

FAUST.
>How is it that they never give up hope?
>Here is a man who clings for his very life
>to everything that is shallow, digging greedily
>in the earth for treasures, and rejoices
>when he finds an earthworm in the earth!
>
>What right has a human voice to speak here?
>And especially the voice of such a dreary pedant?
>Here where the air around me teemed with spirits!
>
>Still, I thank you this once,
>you sorriest of all earth's creatures.
>You wrenched me from a despair
>that was close to destroying me.
>An apparition so vast it dwarfed me!
>A nothing!
>
>I, image of the Godhead!
>I, so certain I would look into the mirror
>of eternal truth! Already basking
>in the pristine light of heaven's glory,
>trailing mortality behind me!

What a fool!

Thinking myself greater than angelic cherubim,
able unhindered to flow through Nature's veins
and revel in the act of creation like the gods!

Ah, but the punishment!
One thundering word has brought me to my knees.

Equal to you?
No.
The power to summon you here?
Yes.

Yes, that I had.

But not the power to hold you.

O that moment!
That supreme moment
when at once I felt so great and so small!
And then to be thrust back, ruthlessly, into uncertainty,
the fated lot of man.

Who will teach me?
What must I shun?
Do I deny my urge,
my quest to seek the source of all life?

Ah, not only the deeds we *do*,
but those done *to* us,
turn us from our goal.

FIT TO BE TIED

Nicky Silver

Present, New York
Arloc, 20s – 30s

Arloc addresses the audience, quite agitated.

ARLOC. DON'T JUDGE ME!! So, I did something terrible?! So what? Everyone's done *something* terrible at some time, haven't they? — and it's not as if I murdered someone or something!!

I suppose I should introduce myself. I'm Arloc Simpson, but a lot of you probably recognize me from the papers. I was in the papers quite a bit when I was younger. It was terrible. It was after my father died. He was very, very wealthy (his father invented frozen food or something, I don't know. I never knew him and I never paid attention). In any event, my father was rich. And when he died, I was twelve at the time, he left all his money to me, *not* my mother. He left her nothing, which pissed her off no end. You'll probably recognize her later too. The point is, he left it all to me and she sued me — or the estate actually, but it felt like me — and lost. So our pictures were in the paper and people stared at us wherever we went — OH, JUDGE ME IF YOU WANT! I DON'T CARE — I didn't plan to do it — well, obviously I did plan it — I mean, I bought equipment. I bought supplies — but I didn't plan it for very long. It's not as if I worked it out over years or anything. The idea just sort of occurred to me one day. It came to me and then before I knew it, it was done. Do you understand?

I'm not arguing insanity. I don't think I was insane. I don't think I am now either — appearances to the contrary. I was perhaps depressed. I'll agree to that: I was depressed. You see, before "this," incident, I think I only ever *cared for* one other person. And he cared for me. I believe he did. I choose to. Do you understand? And then he died and I will hate him forever. I don't mean that. Yes, I do.

In any event, I think that's when this started. The morning I found out that Anthony died. No one called me. I read it in the paper. And I knew AT ONCE I was in trouble! I knew I'd made a mistake! But before Anthony, I had waited forever. I had waited MY WHOLE LIFE to be with someone, to let someone look at me! And I did NOT care what was dangerous! I DIDN'T CARE about myself! About me! I ONLY CARED THAT I HAD WAITED FOREVER! . . . It started that night, when I read he was gone. I couldn't sleep. My muscles hurt. I read Anthony's obituary over and over again in my head — PNEUMONIA is a code word when you read it in the paper! I'M NOT STUPID! . . . I offered up my blood at noon and met my mother for lunch at twelve thirty.

FIT TO BE TIED

Nicky Silver

Present, New York
Arloc, 20s – 30s

Arloc talks about the man of his dreams.

ARLOC. He was beautiful! He was to me! To me, he was! I had to see him. I had to tell him. I wanted to look at him all the time! I had to touch him! I had to smell him! I had to hear him say my name! BUT I DIDN'T MEAN TO DO ANYTHING WRONG! I walked every day! Every night! Surrounded by families, not speaking English, squalling children, smelling sticky, not understanding, never noticing what was in front of them! I understood — I watched the way he moved! I watched his hands in the air, floating, flying, swooping in the sky made of blue construction paper. And every time I left my home I passed IT — that envelope that held my fate — I saw him everywhere! He was everywhere I looked! Him, with no name! Him with soft hair! Him with his lips and his voice! Him loving me! And every night, alone in my bed, WE made love! And I whispered his name into my pillow — Sean, Philip, Daniel, Danny, Dan — I started to prepare!

THE GLASS MENAGERIE

Tennessee Williams

1940s, St. Louis
Tom, any age

Tom talks about how the gentleman caller came about.

TOM. After the fiasco at Rubicam's Business College, the idea of getting a gentleman caller for my sister Laura began to play a more and more important part in my mother's calculations. It become an obsession. Like some archetype of the universal unconscious, the image of the gentleman caller haunted our small apartment. An evening at home rarely passed without some allusion to this image, this spectre, this hope. . . . And even when he wasn't mentioned, his presence hung in my mother's preoccupied look and in my sister's frightened, apologetic manner. It hung like a sentence passed upon the Wingfields! But my mother was a woman of action as well as words. She began to take logical steps in the planned direction. Late that winter and in the early spring — realizing that extra money would be needed to properly feather the nest and plume the bird — she began a vigorous campaign on the telephone, roping in subscribers to one of those magazines for matrons called "The Homemaker's Companion," the type of journal that features the serialized sublimations of ladies of letters who think in terms of delicate cup-like breasts, slim, tapering waists, rich creamy thighs, eyes like wood-smoke in autumn, fingers that soothe and caress like soft, soft strains of music. Bodies as powerful as Estrucan sculpture.

THE GLASS MENAGERIE

Tennessee Williams

1940s, St. Louis
Tom, any age

Tom tells us about how he never really left Laura behind.

TOM. I didn't go to the moon. I went much farther. For time is the longest distance between two places. . . . I left Saint Louis. I descended these steps of this fire-escape for the last time and followed, from then on, in my father's footsteps, attempting to find in motion what was lost in space. . . . I travelled around a great deal. The cities swept about me like dead leaves, leaves that were brightly colored but torn away from the branches. I would have stopped, but I was pursued by something. It always came upon me unawares, taking me altogether by surprise. Perhaps it was a familiar bit of music. Perhaps it was only a piece of transparent glass. . . . Perhaps I am walking along a street at night, in some strange city, before I have found companions, and I pass the lighted window of a shop where perfume is sold. The window is filled with pieces of colored glass, tiny transparent bottles in delicate colors, like bits of a shattered rainbow. Then all at once my sister touches my shoulder. I turn around and look into her eyes. . . . Oh, Laura, Laura, I tried to leave you behind me, but I am more faithful than I intended to be! I reach for a cigarette, I cross the street, I run into a movie or a bar. I buy a drink, I speak to the nearest stranger — anything that can blow your candles out! — for nowadays the world is lit by lightning! Blow out your candles, Laura . . .

THE GOODBYE PEOPLE
Herb Gardner

1970s, New York
Arthur, 40s

Arthur calls the NY Times *because the sun didn't rise when they said it would.*

ARTHUR. Goddamn *New York Times . . . (Going quickly to phone booths.)* Who ya supposed to believe any more? Who ya supposed to trust? *(Speaks into phone.)* Hello, *New York Times?* I think we got a problem here. We got a definite problem here. Your Late City Edition says here, page 70, column 3: "February 22; sunrise: 6:41." O.K., well it's six forty-*eight* right now, and I don't know what's happening up in *your* neighborhood, lady, but down here we got darkness . . . Well, if you're just the operator, then who's responsible, who's on top of the sunrise situation over there? . . . City Desk? Fine. Lemme speak to them . . . Who's this? Mr. Mallory? Mr. Mallory, look out your window. What do ya see? That's called darkness, Mr. Mallory. That's nighttime you got goin' on out there. My name is Arthur Korman, a regular subscriber to your publication, come at great inconvenience to myself to witness the birth of a new day, come on the B.M.T. in quest of beauty and gettin' my ass froze off in total blackness down here! What the hell're you guys usin' for weather information up there? What're ya, a buncha *gypsies* up there!

HAMLET

William Shakespeare

Hamlet, 20s – 30s

Hamlet plots.

HAMLET. How all occasions do inform against me.
       And spur my dull revenge! What is a man,
       If his chief good and market of his time
       Be but to sleep and feed? a beast, no more.
       Sure he that made us with such large discourse,
       Looking before and after, gave us not
       That capability and godlike reason
       To fust in us unus'd. Now, whether it be
       Bestial oblivion or craven scruple
       Of thinking too precisely on the event, —
       A thought which, quarter'd, hath but one part wisdom
       And ever three parts coward, — I do not know
       Why yet I live to say, *This thing's to do;* sith I have cause and
              will, and strength, and means
       To do't. Examples, gross as earth, exhort me.
       Witness this army, of such mass and charge
       Led by a delicate and tender prince;
       Whose spirit, with divine ambition puff'd,
       Makes mouths at the invisible event;
       Exposing what is mortal and unsure
       To all that fortune, death, and danger dare,
       Even for an egg-shell. Rightly to be great
       Is not to stir without great argument,
       But greatly to find quarrel in a straw
       When honour's at the stake. How stand I, then,
       That have a father kill'd, a mother stain'd,
       Excitements of my reason and my blood,
       And let all sleep? while, to my shame, I see

The imminent death of twenty thousand men,
That, for a fantasy and trick of fame,
Go to their graves like beds; fight for a plot
Whereon the numbers cannot try the cause,
Which is not tomb enough and continent
To hide the slain? — O, from this time forth,
My thoughts be bloody, or be nothing worth!

HARVEY

Mary Chase

Present, American West
Elwood, any age

Elwood goes to the phone and calls Dr. Chumley looking for Harvey.

ELWOOD. Hello, Chumley's Rest? Is Doctor Chumley there? Oh —
it's Mrs. Chumley! This is Elwood P. Dowd speaking. How are you
tonight? Tell me, Mrs. Chumley, were you able to locate Harvey? —
Don't worry about it. I'll find him. I'm sorry I missed you at the McClure
cocktail party. The people were all charming and I was able to leave quite
a few of my cards. I waited until you phoned and said you couldn't come
because a patient had escaped. Where am I? I'm here. But I'm leaving
right away. I must find Harvey. Well, goodbye, Mrs. Chumley. My re-
gards to you and anybody else you happen to run into. Goodbye.

HEAVEN
George Walker

Present, American City
Jimmy, 20s

Jimmy tells us his story.

JIMMY. Yeah, thanks. But where was I. Oh yeah. Pain. It's all about pain. Unbearable soul-sucking pain. And what we do to escape it. But first, speaking of sucking. And this might be related to pain. But anyway when I was a teenager I was busted for possession and somehow I managed to keep my parents from finding out. And I go to court by myself to take whatever enlightened punishment is gonna be doled out to me for the mortal sin of having two reefers in my jean jacket. But because I'm nervous and my cure for that was always to get pretty wasted, I take some mescaline I've had stashed away for awhile and I find myself sitting at the back of the courtroom, my mind drifting towards the outskirts of reality. Sweating. Vibrating. And then suddenly a voice from the front announces that some guy's been charged with sucking on a cannibal's dick. And immediately a whole bunch of stuff races through my head. First. Why is that a crime. Second. Why wasn't I told that cannibals were living around here. And also, if this guy really was a cannibal wouldn't sucking on his dick be kind of a dangerous thing to do. As in, "Thanks for the blowjob. Boy am I ever hungry." Anyway I'm tormenting myself with all these questions when somehow it gets through the matted fucking mess which is my brain that the guy is actually charged with marijuana use. And that some uptight narc has been up there describing this horror as "sucking on a cannabis stick." Okay so I've got it straight now. But I'm haunted by my initial response. And the image of a huge black man getting blown by this pimply undergraduate in the defendant's seat. First why is the guy in my brain black. And second why is he huge. And the only answer I can come up with is . . . I must be a racist.

THE HOLOGRAM THEORY

Jessica Goldberg

Present, New York,
Simon, 40s

Simon in his study speaks with a friend on the phone about his son.

SIMON. My fucking son. You understand me, Jeff? Goddamnit. What can I do? It kills me. Really. You can't fucking control anything, shit. Don't ever have kids, I'm telling you now. It's not drugs this time. No, not robbery. I think, shit, I think we may have, I can't even say it, killed someone. Wow. I can't even understand that. How could that be? How could . . . Just tell me it's not my fault. What the fuck did I do? Okay, you're right, forget the past. Let's think about the future, the future. Send him to Europe, good, boarding school. He's not really a son, he's a liability. The details . . . you ask him the details, tell them to me. I can handle them better coming from your mouth. Hold on, let me get him. *(Calling.)* Julian! Pick up the phone in there. Jeff needs to speak with you. Did he pick up? Julian!! Pick up the phone! No, shit, hold on. *(Simon exits. The phone sits on his desk, moments pass, then finally, Simon returns. He picks up the phone.)* He's gone. He's not in the house. Meaning, he left, out the window, gone. Shit. Fuck Jeff, where is my son?

THE HOUSE OF BLUE LEAVES

John Guare

1960s, New York
Ronnie, 17

Ronnie speaks to us in an innocent, diabolical way.

RONNIE. My father tell you all about me? Pope Ronnie? Charmed life?
How great I am? That's how he is with you. You should hear him with
me, you'd sing a different tune pretty quick, and it wouldn't be "Where
Is the Devil in Evelyn." I was twelve years old and all the newspapers had
headlines on my twelfth birthday that Billy was coming to town. And
Life was doing stories on him and *Look* and the newsreels because Billy
was searching America to find the Ideal American Boy to play Huckleberry Finn. And Billy came to New York and called my father and asked
him if he could stay here — Billy needed a hideout. In Waldorf Astorias
all over the country, chambermaids would wheel silver carts to change
the sheets. And out of the sheets would hop little boys saying, "Hello,
I'm Huckleberry Finn." All over the country, little boys dressed in blue
jeans and straw hats would be sent to him in crates, be under the silver
cover covering his dinner, his medicine cabinet in all his hotel rooms, his
suitcase — "Hello, hello, I'm Huckleberry Finn." And he was coming
here to hide out. Here — Billy coming here — I asked the nun in school
who was Huckleberry Finn —
　　　The nun in Queen of Martyrs knew. She told me. The Ideal American Boy. And coming home, all the store windows reflected me and the
mirror in the tailor shop said, "Hello, Huck." The butcher shop window
said, "Hello, Huck. Hello, Huckleberry Finn. All America wants to meet
Billy and he'll be hiding out in your house." I came home — went in
there — into my room and packed my bag. . . . I knew Billy would see
me and take me back to California with him that very day. This room
smelled of ammonia and air freshener and these slip covers were new that
day and my parents were filling up the icebox in their brand-new clothes,
filling up the icebox with food and liquor as excited as if the Pope was

coming — and nervous because they hadn't seen him in a long while — Billy. They told me my new clothes were on my bed. To go get dressed. I didn't want to tell them I'd be leaving shortly to start a new life. That I'd be flying out to California with Billy on the H.M.S. *Huckleberry*. I didn't want tears from them — only trails of envy. . . . I went to my room and packed my bag and waited.

The doorbell rang. If you listen close, you can still hear the echoes of those wet kisses and handshakes and tears and backs getting hit and "Hello, Billy's, hello." They talked for a long time about people from their past. And then my father called out: "Ronnie, guess who? Billy, we named him after your father. Ronnie, guess who?"

I picked up my bag and said Goodbye to myself in the mirror. Came out. Billy there. Smiling.

It suddenly dawned on me. You had to do things to get parts.

I began dancing. And singing. Immediately. Things I have never done in my life — before or since. I stood on my head and skipped and whirled — spectacular leaps in the air so I could see veins in the ceiling — ran up and down the keys of the piano and sang and began laughing and crying soft and loud to show off all my emotions. And I heard music and drums that I couldn't even keep up with. And then cut off all my emotions just like that. Instantly. And took a deep bow like the Dying Swan I saw on Ed Sullivan. I picked up my suitcase and waited by the door.

Billy turned to my parents, whose jaws were down to about there, and Billy said, "You never told me you had a mentally retarded child. You never told me I had an idiot for a godchild," and I picked up my bag and went into my room and shut the door and never came out the whole time he was there.

My only triumph was he could never find a Huckleberry Finn. Another company made the picture a few years later, but it flopped.

My father thinks I'm nothing. Billy. My sergeant. They laugh at me. You laughing at me? I'm going to fool you all. By tonight, I'll be on the headlines all over the world. Cover of *Time. Life.* TV specials. I hope they use this picture of me — I look better with hair — Go ahead — laugh. Because you know what I think of you?

I NEVER SANG FOR MY FATHER

Robert Anderson

Present, New York
Gene, 40s

Gene tells about his last visit in his father's house.

GENE. That night I left my Father's house forever . . . I took the first right and the second left . . . and this time I went as far as California. . . .

Peggy and I visited him once or twice . . . and then he came to California to visit us, and had a fever and swollen ankles, and we put him in a hospital, and he never left. . . . The reason we gave, and which he could accept, for not leaving . . . the swollen ankles. But the real reason . . . the arteries were hardening, and gradually over several years slipped into complete and speechless senility . . . with all his life centered in his burning eyes.

IN THE BLOOD

Susan Lori Parks

Now, Here
Reverend D, 30s – 40s

Reverend D, practices his preaching, while cleaning his cornerstone, a white block of granite with the date in Roman numerals on it.

REVEREND D. — "It is easier for a camel to go through the eye of a needle than for a rich man to enter the kingdom of God." And you hear that and you say, let me get a tax shelter and hide some of my riches so that when I stand up there in judgment, God wont be none the wiser! And that is the problem with the way we see God. For most of us, God is like the IRS. God garnishes yr wages if you don't pay up. God withholds. The wages of sin, they lead to death, so you say, let me give to the poor. But not any poor, just those respectable charities. I want my poor looking good. I want my poor to know that it was me who bought the such and such. I want my poor on tv. I want famous poor, not miscellaneous poor. And I don't want local poor. Local poor dont look good. Gimmie foreign poor. Poverty exotica. Gimmie brown and yellow skins against a non-western landscape, some savanna, some rainforest, some rice paddy. Gimmie big sad eyes with the berri-berri belly and the outstretched hands struggling to say "Thank-You" the only english they know, right into the camera. And put me up there with them, holding them, comforting them, telling them everythings gonna be alright, we gonna raise you up, we gonna get you on the bandwagon of our ways, put a smile in yr heart and a hamburger in yr belly, baby.

THE JEW OF MALTA
Christopher Marlowe

1500s, Malta
Barabas, any age

Barabas talks to us about the importance of money.

BARABAS. So that of thus much that return was made:
    And of the third part of the Persian ships,
    There was the venture summed and satisfied.
    As for those Samnites, and the men of Uz,
    That bought my Spanish oils, and wines of Greece,
    Here have I pursed their paltry silverings.
    Fie; what a trouble 'tis to count this trash.
    Well fare the Arabians, who so richly pay
    The things they traffic for with wedge of gold,
    Whereof a man may easily in a day
    Tell that which may maintain him all his life.
    The needy groom that never fingered groat,
    Would make a miracle of thus much coin:
    But he whose steel-barred coffers are crammed full,
    And all his lifetime hath been tired,
    Wearying his fingers' ends with telling it,
    Would in his age be loath to labour so,
    And for a pound to sweat himself to death:
    Give me the merchants of the Indian mines,
    That trade in metal of the purest mould;
    The wealthy Moor, that in the Eastern rocks
    Without control can pick his riches up,
    And in his house heap pearl like pebble-stones;
    Receive them free, and sell them by the weight,
    Bags of fiery opals, sapphires, amethysts,
    Jacinths, hard topaz, grass-green emeralds,
    Beauteous rubies, sparkling diamonds,

And seldseen costly stones of so great price,
As one of them indifferently rated,
And of a caract of this quantity,
May serve in peril of calamity
To ransom great kings from captivity.
This is the ware wherein consists my wealth:
And thus methinks should men of judgement frame
Their means of traffic from the vulgar trade,
And as their wealth increaseth, so inclose
Infinite riches in a little room.
But now how stands the wind?
Into what corner peers my halcyon's bill?
Ha, to the east? Yes: see how stands the vanes?
East and by south: why then I hope my ships
I sent for Egypt and the bordering isles
Are gotten up by Nilus' winding banks:
Mine argosy from Alexandria,
Loaden with spice and silks, now under sail,
Are smoothly gliding down by Candy shore
To Malta, through our Mediterranean sea.
But who comes here? How now.

THE JEW OF MALTA

Christopher Marlowe

1500s, Malta
Barabas, any age

Barabas speaks to us about his riches.

BARABAS. Thus trowls our fortune in by land and sea,
       And thus are we on every side enriched:
       These are the blessings promised to the Jews,
       And herein was old Abram's happiness:
       What more may heaven do for earthly man
       Than thus to pour out plenty in their laps,
       Ripping the bowels of the earth for them,
       Making the sea their servant, and the winds
       To drive their substance with successful blasts?
       Who hateth me but for me happiness?
       Or who is honoured now but for his wealth?
       Rather had I a Jew be hated thus,
       Than pitied in a Christian poverty:
       For I can see no fruits in all their faith,
       But malice, falsehood, and excessive pride,
       Which methinks fits not their profession.
       Happily some hapless man hath conscience,
       And for his conscience lives in beggary.
       They say we are a scattered nation:
       I cannot tell, but we have scambled up
       More wealth by far than those that brag of faith.
       There's Kirriah Jairim, the great Jew of Greece,
       Obed in Bairseth, Nones in Portugal,
       Myself in Malta, some in Italy,
       Many in France, and wealthy every one:
       Ay, wealthier far than any Christian.
       I must confess we come not to be kings:

That's not our fault: alas, our number's few,
And crowns come either by succession,
Or urged by force; and nothing violent,
Oft have I heard tell, can be permanent.
Give us a peaceful rule, make Christians kings,
That thirst so much for principality.
I have no charge, nor many children,
But one sole daughter, whom I hold as dear
As Agamemnon did his Iphigen:
And all I have is hers. But who comes here?

JIMMY SHINE
Murray Schisgal

Present, New York
Jimmy, 20s

Jimmy, after thoroughly cleaning his apartment, rehearses a future date with Elizabeth.

JIMMY. Sparkling. Never has the Shine apartment sparkled like it sparkles today. *(He looks in the mirror.)* Hello, there, you handsome devil you. Not looking too bad this morning. Eyes a bit creased around the corners, but still young, still have a ways to go before it all falls apart, before it all . . . *(His body slowly bends and he takes on the posture and voice of an old man. He moves to the door playing an imaginary scene.)* Is that you there now, Elizabeth? Oh, one second, I'll be right there. Be patient . . . Legs a bit stiff this morning . . . Come in, Elizabeth, come in. *(Opening imaginary door.)* Oh, my Elizabeth. I am so glad you could come today. No, no, it's all right. I haven't been waiting too long. But let me look at you, my dear . . . You seem to have lost all your hair . . . no matter, no matter. . . . Oh no, it is not the waiting that has upset me. It is my passion. My passion seems to have slipped down to my knees, and our first attempts at love-making may be a little awkward, but no matter, my dear, we will work it out. Oh my dear, let us make love now, right now . . . But first you must excuse me: I must go to the bathroom . . . I'm ready for you now, Elizabeth. I'm waiting and ready, Elizabeth Evans . . . Elizabeth Evans Leon . . .

KING LEAR

William Shakespeare

Edmund, 20s – 30s

Edmund explains why he is the way he is.

EDMUND. This is the excellent foppery of the world, that, when we are sick in fortune, — often the surfeit of our own behavior — we make guilty of our disasters the sun, the moon, and the stars: as if we were villains by necessity; fools by heavenly compulsion; knaves, thieves, and treachers by spherical predominance; drunkards, liars, and adulterers by an enforced obedience of planetary influence; and all that we are evil in, by a divine thrusting on: an admirable evasion of whoremaster man, to lay his goatish disposition to the charge of a star! My father compounded with my mother under the dragon's tail, and my nativity was under *ursa major;* so that it follows I am rough and lecherous. — Tut, I should have been that I am, had the maidenliest star in the firmament twinkled on my bastardizing.

KING LEAR
William Shakespeare

Fool, any age

The Fool decides to share a bit of prophecy with the audience.

FOOL. This is a brave night to cool a courtezan. —
    I'll speak a prophecy ere I go: —
    When priests are more in word than matter;
    When brewers mar their malt with water;
    When nobles are their tailors' tutors;
    No heretics burn'd, but wenches' suitors;
    When every case in law is right;
    No squire in debt, nor no poor knight;
    When slanders do not live in tongues;
    Nor cutpurses come not to throngs;
    When userers tell their gold i'the field;
    And bawds and whores do churches build; —
    Then shall the realm of Albion
    Come to great confusion:
    Then comes the time, who lives to see't,
    That going shall be us'd with feet.
    This prophecy Merlin shall make; for I live before his time.

LIFE AND LIMB
Keith Reddin

1950s, American City
Franklin, 20s

Franklin talks about how dangerous situations affect him.

FRANKLIN. Freud, in his dynamics of the personality defines the concept of reality anxiety as a painful emotional experience resulting from a perception of danger in the external world. A danger is any condition of the environment which threatens to harm the person. My favorite movie is the movie "The Bridges of Toko Ri" starring William Holden, Mickey Rooney and Grace Kelly. Also I was sexually aroused during certain sequences in "The Creature From the Black Lagoon," but I have never related this information to anyone. I noticed I was rooting for the Creature to attack this girl scientist and one scene where he is swimming under her, following her slowly while she is unaware of his presence gave me an erection. I looked around at this point in the movie and noticed that quite a few men in the audience had strange expressions on their faces also. Experiences that overpower one with anxiety are called "traumatic" because they reduce the person to an infantile state of helplessness. The prototype of all traumatic experiences is the birth trauma. The newly-born baby is bombarded with excessive stimulation from the world for which its fetal experience has not prepared it.

A 3-D sequel to "The Creature From the Black Lagoon" was released the next year due to the success of the original film, but I stayed away from that fearing what the consequences of three dimensional projection could cause me.

Effie and Doina never made it back from the movies that afternoon. The balcony of the Fox Theatre under which they were sitting enjoying a 2:30 showing of "Cattle Queen of Montana" starring Barbara Stanwick and Ronald Reagan collapsed, killing them instantly. The surprise I had for Effie was a new television. While she and Doina were at the movies,

I moved all the furniture around the apartment to find a place to set this new television. I was informed by the police about the accident at 4:35, she had been pronounced dead on arrival. I sent the TV back the next day. I didn't even plug it in.

LOVERS
Brian Friel

Present, Ireland
Andy, 20s – 30s

Andy tells us about his father-in-law.

ANDY. I'll tell you something; I see damn all through these things. Well, I mean, there's damn all to see in a back yard. Now and again maybe a sparrow or something like that lands on top of the wall there, but it's so close it's only a blur. Anyway, most of the time I sit with my eyes closed. And Hanna — she probably knows I do 'cause she's no dozer; but once I come out here — I'll say that for her — she leaves me alone. A gesture I make, and she — you know — she respects it. Maybe because her aul fella used to do the same thing; for that's where I learned the dodge. As a matter of fact these are his glasses. And this is where he was found dead, the poor bugger, just three years ago, slumped in a chair out here, and him all wrapped up in his cap and his top coat and his muffler and his woolen gloves. Wait — I'm telling you a lie. Four years ago — aye — that's more like it, 'cause he passed away that January Hanna and me started going, and we won't be married four years until next summer. Not that I knew the man, beyond bidding him the time of day there. Maybe he'd be inside in the kitchen there or more likely sitting out here, and I'd say to him, "Hello there, Mr. Wilson" — you know the way, when you're going with a woman, you try to be affable to her aul fella — and he'd say, "Oh, hello there, Andy" or something like that back. But you know yourself a man that's looking through binoculars, you don't like interrupting him. Civil wee man he was, too. Fifty years a stoker out in the general hospital. And a funny thing — one of the male nurses out there was telling me — all his life he stuck to the night shift; worked all night and slept all day, up there in that room above the kitchen. Peculiar, eh? All his life. Never saw the wife except for maybe a couple of hours in the evening. Never saw Hanna, the daughter, except at the weekends. Funny, eh? And yet by all accounts the civilest and decentest wee man you could meet. Funny, too. And the way things turn out in life; when the mother-in-law found him out here about seven o'clock that evening, she got such a bloody fright that she collapsed and took to the bed for good and hasn't risen since, not even the morning we got married. The heart. But that's another story. Anyway, Hanna and me, as I say, we were only started going at the time; and then with the aul fella dying and the aul woman taking to the bed, like we couldn't go to the pictures nor dances nor nothing like any other couple; so I started coming here every evening. And this is where we done our courting, in there, on the couch.

M. BUTTERFLY

David Henry Hwang

1960s, Beijing
Gallimard, any age

Gallimard talks about his wife.

GALLIMARD. My wife's innocent question kept ringing in my ears. I asked around, but no one knew anything about the Chinese opera. It took four weeks, but my curiosity overcame my cowardice. This Chinese diva — this unwilling Butterfly — what did she do to make her so proud?

The room was hot, and full of smoke. Wrinkled faces, old women, teeth missing — a man with a growth on his neck, like a human toad. All smiling, pipes falling from their mouths, cracking nuts between their teeth, a live chicken pecking at my foot — all looking, screaming, gawking . . . at her.

M. BUTTERFLY

David Henry Hwang

1960s, Beijing
Gallimard, any age

We hear about what happened in China.

GALLIMARD. And then, China began to change. Mao became very old, and his cult became very strong. And, like many old men, he entered his second childhood. So he handed over the reins of state to those with minds like his own. And children ruled the Middle Kingdom with complete caprice. The doctrine of the Cultural Revolution implied continuous anarchy. Contact between Chinese and foreigners became impossible. Our flat was confiscated. Her fame and my money now counted against us. And somehow the American war went wrong too. Four hundred thousand dollars were being spent for every Viet Cong killed; so General Westmoreland's remark that the Oriental does not value life the way Americans do was oddly accurate. Why weren't the Vietnamese people giving in? Why were they content instead to die and die and die again?

THE MARRIAGE OF FIGARO

Pierre Beaumarchais, translated by Richard Nelson

1700s, Spain
Figaro, 20s – 30s

Figaro can't believe what a fool he has been.

FIGARO. O woman! woman! woman! You weak deceitful creature. As each beast must be true to its nature, is it the nature of the beast, woman, to deceive? . . . After flatly refusing, in the presence of her mistress, when I urged it, after giving me her word, then while giving me her word, then while giving me her hand! . . . He's laughing while he reads; what a monster and me, what a fool! . . . No, Sir, you will not have her . . . you will not have her. Because you're a lord you think you're God's gift to the world! . . .

Nobility, wealth, position; because of these you think you can do as you want. But how have you earned any of this? You suffered a little when you were born, that's about it. Inside, you're nothing much. But goddamnit, the same can't be said for me! Thrown alone into the black sea of humanity, I survived on more wit and cunning than has been used to rule all of Spain for the past one hundred years! And you want to tangle with me! . . . Someone's coming! . . . It's her . . .

THE MERCHANT OF VENICE

William Shakespeare

Launcelot, 20s – 30s

Launcelot can't decide whether to run from his master or to stay by his side.

LAUNCELOT. Certainly my conscience will serve me to run from this Jew, my master. The fiend is at mine elbow, and tempts me, saying to me, *Gobbo, Launcelot Gobbo, good Launcelot, or good Gobbo, or good Launcelot Gobbo, use your legs, take the start, run away.* My conscience says, — *No; take heed, honest Launcelot; take heed, honest Gobbo; or* as aforesaid, *honest Launcelot Gobbo; do not run, scorn running with thy heels.* Well, the most courageous fiend bids me pack: *Via!* says the fiend; *away!* says the fiend, *for the heavens; rouse up a brave mind,* says the fiend, *and run.* Well, my conscience, hanging about the neck of my heart, says very wisely to me, — *My honest friend, Launcelot, being an honest man's son,* or rather an honest woman's son; — for indeed, my father did something smack, something grow to, he had a kind of taste; — well, my conscience says, *Launcelot, budge not. Budge,* says the fiend. *Budge not,* says my conscience. Conscience, say I, you counsel well; fiend, say I, you counsel well: to be ruled by my conscience, I should stay with the Jew, my master, who (God bless the mark!) is a kind of devil; and, to run away from the Jew, I should be ruled by the fiend, who, saving your reverence, is the devil himself. Certainly the Jew is the very devil incarnation: and, in my conscience, my conscience is but a kind of hard conscience, to offer to counsel me to stay with the Jew. The fiend gives the more friendly counsel: I will run, fiend; my heels are at your commandment; I will run.

MUCH ADO ABOUT NOTHING
William Shakespeare

Benedick, 20s – 30s

Benedick expresses his feelings of disgust toward Claudio's new behaviour.

BENEDICK. I do much wonder that one man, seeing how much another man is a fool when he dedicates his behaviours to love, will, after he hath laughed at such shallow follies in others, become the argument of his own scorn by falling in love: and such a man is Claudio. I have known when there was no music with him but the drum and the fife, and now had he rather hear the tabor and the pipe. I have known when he would have walked ten mile afoot to see a good armour, and now will he lie ten nights awake carving the fashion of a new doublet. He was wont to speak plain and to the purpose, like an honest man and a soldier, and now is he turned orthography — his words are a very fantastical banquet, just so many strange dishes. May I be so converted and see with these eyes? I cannot tell; I think not. I will not be sworn but love may transform me to an oyster, but I'll take my oath on it, till he have made an oyster of me, he shall never make me such a fool. One woman is fair, yet I am well; another is wise, yet I am well; another virtuous, yet I am well; but till all graces be in one woman, one woman shall not come in my grace. Rich she shall be, that's certain; wise, or I'll none; virtuous, or I'll never cheapen her; fair, or I'll never look on her; mild, or come not near me; noble, or not I for an angel; of good discourse, an excellent musician, and her hair shall be — of what colour it please God. Ha! the Prince and Monsieur Love! I will hide me in the arbour.

MY CHILDREN, MY AFRICA

Athol Fugard

1980s, South Africa
Mr. M., 50s – 60s

Mr. M. explains to us why hope can be dangerous.

MR. M. Look at me! I'm sweating today. I've been sweating for a week. Why? Because one of those animals, the one called Hope, has broken loose and is looking for food. Don't be fooled by its gentle name. It is as dangerous as Hate and Despair would be if they ever managed to break out. You think I'm exaggerating? Pushing my metaphor a little too far? Then I'd like to put you inside a black skin and ask you to keep Hope alive, find food for it on these streets where our children, our loved and precious children go hungry and die of malnutrition. No, believe me, it is a dangerous animal for a black man to have prowling around in his heart. So how do I manage to keep mine alive, you ask? Friends, I am going to let you in on a terrible secret. That is why I am a teacher.

MY CHILDREN, MY AFRICA
Athol Fugard

1980s, South Africa
Mr. M., 50s – 60s

Mr. M. talks to us about Confucius and how his beliefs have affected his life.

MR. M. "I am a man who in eager pursuit of knowledge forgets his food and in the joy of its attainment forgets his sorrow, and who does not perceive that old age is coming on." No. As I'm sure you have already guessed, that is not me. My pursuit of knowledge is eager, but I do perceive, and only too clearly, that old age is coming on, and at the best of times I do a bad job of forgetting my sorrows. Those wonderful words come from the finest teacher I have ever had, that most wise of all the ancient philosophers . . . Confucius! Yes. I am a Confucian. A black Confucian! There are not many of us. In fact I think there's a good chance that the only one in the country is talking to you at this moment.

I claim him as my teacher because I have read very carefully, and many times, and I will read it many times more, a little book I have about him, his life, his thoughts and utterances. Truly, they *are* wonderful words, my friends, wonderful, wonderful words! My classroom motto comes from its pages: "Learning undigested by thought is labor lost, Thought unassisted by learning is perilous!" But the words that challenge me most these days, is something he said towards the end of his life. At the age of seventy he turned to his pupils once a day and said that he could do whatever his heart prompted, without transgressing what was right.

What do you say to that?

Think about it. *Anything* his heart prompted, *anything* that rose up as a spontaneous urge in his soul, *without* transgressing what was right!

What a heart, my friends! Aren't you envious of old Confucius? Wouldn't it be marvelous to have a heart you could trust like that? Imagine being able to wake up in the morning in your little room, yawn and stretch, scratch a few flea bites and then jump out of your bed and eat your bowl of mealie-pap and sour milk with a happy heart because you know that when you walk out into the world you will be free to obey and act out, with a clear conscience, all the promptings of your heart. No matter what you see out there on the battle grounds of location streets, and believe me, there are days now when my eyesight feels more like a curse than a blessing, no matter what stories of hardship and suffering you hear, or how bad the news you read in the newspaper, knowing that the whole truth, which can't be printed, is even worse . . . in spite of all that, you need have no fear of your spontaneous urges, because in obeying them you will not transgress what is right.

OTHELLO
William Shakespeare

Iago, 20s – 30s

Iago plans his revenge against Othello.

IAGO. Thus do I ever make my fool my purse;
    For I mine own gain'd knowledge should profane
    If I would time expend to such a snipe
    But for my sport and profit. I hate the Moor;
    And it is thought abroad that 'twixt my sheets
    He has done my office: I know not if't be true;
    But I, for mere suspicion in that kind,
    Will do as if for surety. He holds me well;
    The better shall my purpose work on him.
    Cassio's a proper man: let me see now;
    To get his place, and to plume up my will
    In double knavery, — How, how? — Let's see: —
    After some time to abuse Othello's ear
    That he is too familiar with his wife: —
    He hath a person, and a smooth dispose,
    To be suspected; fram'd to make women false.
    The Moor is of a free and open nature,
    That thinks men honest that but seem to be so;
    And will as tenderly be led by the nose
    As asses are.
    I haven't; — it is engender'd: — hell and night
    Must bring this monstrous birth to the
    World's light.

THE OWL AND THE PUSSYCAT
Bill Manhoff

1970s, New York
Felix, 20s – 30s

Felix arrives home at two A.M.

FELIX. *(Addressing the bedroom door as he crosses to it.)* I see you couldn't find a room again. I should have known you were lying. What made me think you'd keep your word? You don't know how to — *(He has exited to bedroom on the last words. There's a pause. From offstage.)* Doris! Doris — ? *(*Felix *comes slowly out of the bedroom. He goes to the closet door, opens it, looks inside; closes the door.* Doris *has gone. He goes to the sofa, sits, looking at the TV set. The PHONE rings. He reaches for it and pulls back; he rises and lights a cigarette nervously as the PHONE continues to ring. It's a slow patient ring with all the time in the world. Finally* Felix *picks it up with an impulsive swoop. Angry; into phone.)* Hello — Oh — nothing, Victor — I just got home. — I went to a movie. . . . Angry? — Why should I get angry at a telephone? Helpless tool of a monopoly! What? . . . Oh — when did she call? What was the number? 4-6792. Goodnight. *(Hangs up. He paces, miserable. He stops at the phone, picks it up, picks up the phone number, puts it down. Picks it up again and dials; waits. He hears* Doris *say "Hello" and he panics.)* Wrong number. *(He slams the receiver down and paces, dials, waits, and panics once more.)* Wrong number! *(Slams down the receiver. He's so angry with himself he slaps his face hard enough to stagger himself. Then gathers all his courage. Deliberately and resolutely picks up the phone and dials.)* Hello, Doris? . . . Felix. I hope I didn't wake you. . . . No! Wrong numbers, huh? . . . That's a shame. I guess at this hour of the morning there's an awful lot of drunk dialing. Drunk dialing! You know, like drunk driving — it's a joke. I know there's nothing funny about drunk driving. That isn't what I meant — Oh, forget it. Well I just got home. You left your television set . . . Oh . . . Tell him to come after three . . . How do you like your room? That's a shame! Well, don't let it depress you — you'll be on your

89

feet again in no time . . . No, it was not a crack! You mustn't be so damn sensitive . . . All right, all right. Listen I've been doing a lot of thinking and I wanted to talk to you. . . . Not on the phone . . . Well, I've been thinking and I realized that we got off on the wrong foot, you and I, and it was silly and I think we can be friends and I think our relationship must be re-established on a different basis . . . No. They just sound big over the phone. Look, I thought if you weren't doing anything right now . . . *(He gets a disappointing response to this.)* Oh . . . yes — well how about having lunch with me? . . . Oh . . . well what are you doing for — ? . . . I see. Yes . . . Yes . . . That won't give us much time . . . Yes. All right, I'll look for you around six . . . I hope you don't . . . Doris? . . . Hello . . . Doris? *(Doris has hung up.)*

PEER GYNT

Henrik Ibsen, translated by Paul Green

1800s, Norway
Peer, 20s – 30s

Peer suddenly awakes, jumps to his feet and looks about him in waking dismay and horror. He realizes what is happening and runs wildly up and down screaming.

PEER. They are stealing my gold. No — no — it's a dream. I'm asleep. A dream — it's got to be a dream. No — it's the truth. They're putting to sea. Scoundrels — thieves — God up there — Our father Who art in Heaven — listen — hear me. This is Peer Gynt — help me, Father — help me, God! Back the engine — lower the gig — Stop 'em, stop 'em — make something go wrong — hear me — hear me — Damn if he hears a thing — He's deaf as usual when He's needed. A fine sort of God you are. I went out of the slave business. I sold my Negro plantation. I sent missionaries to Asia. Well, Sir, one good turn deserves another. Help me — help me — Sunk. Gone to the bottom. Everything — rats, men, all! Praise be to God, I was not on it. I have escaped. I was *meant* to be saved. They were meant to be destroyed. Thank you and bless you for saving me. You've kept an eye on me in spite of my sins. What a wonderful thing to feel that Divine Providence specially protects you. Protect, I say? What was that — a lion growling in the rushes — I am imagining things. Still it's all right to trust in God, but you better keep your powder dry. I'll find me a tree. And I'll sing a couple of hymns for good measure too if I can remember them. Things don't look too promising, Peer Gynt. Anyway, He's got a fatherly feeling for me. I know that. My ship and money gone to the bottom. He's not an economical God, that's a fact. Well, old Number One, you've got to be moving.

PTERODACTYLS

Nicky Silver

Present, Philadelphia
Todd, 20s

Todd addresses the audience, giving us a brief history of the world.

TODD. In the beginning, there were dinosaurs. Lots of dinosaurs. And they were big. They were very, very large — in comparison to man they were. They were huge. And there were many different kinds. There were cerotops and stegosauruses. There was the tyrannosaurus and the ptero- dactyl. And they lived, not in harmony, roaming the earth at will, raping, as it were, the planet and pillaging without regard. And, and um . . . uh. *(He looses his place and quickly checks his pockets for notes.)* Um, I seem to have forgotten my notes. I'm sorry. I thought I left them in my pocket. Maybe I wasn't supposed to wear this. Maybe I left them on the table. Maybe I — oh well, it doesn't matter now. I don't have them. That's the point. I think I remember most of it — Maybe I left them — it doesn't matter. Where was I? Oh, yes. It got cold. That's right, it got very, very cold and all the dinosaurs died. They all died. At once. It got cold and they died. And the land masses shifted and arranged themselves into the pattern we see now on the map. Basically. I think. There weren't any di- visions for countries or states or anything, and I'm sure California was bigger, but it resembled what's on the map. During the cold spell, which is generally referred to as "the ice age" — or maybe it was before the ice age, or after it — I can't remember — but life started spontaneously. In a lake. Here, I think. *(He indicates the Sea of Japan.)* And amoebas multi- plied and became fish — don't ask me how — which evolved into mon- keys. And then one day, the monkeys stood up, erect, realized they had opposing thumbs and developed speech. Thus, Mankind was born. Here. *(He indicates Africa.)* Some people liked Africa, so they stayed there and became black. Some people left, looking for something, and became Europeans. And the Europeans forgot about the Africans and made countries and Queen Elizabeth executed her own half-sister Mary Queen of Scots. Some Europeans were Jewish, but most were Christians of some kind, Jesus having been born some time prior — oops, I forgot that. I'm sorry. Jesus was born. And there were other religions too, but I can't remember much about them, so I'm sure they weren't very important. During the Renaissance people got very fat. Picasso sculpted "David," Marco Polo invented pizza, Columbus discovered the new world and Gaetan Dugas discovered the fountain of youth. Europeans imported tea, to drink, and Africans to do their work. Edison invented the telephone, Martha Graham invented modern dance. Hitler invented fascism and Rose Kennedy invented nepotism. Orson Welles made *Citizen Kane* and mothers loved their children, who rebelled, when the sun shined most of the time, except when it rained and there was a rhythm to our breathing. There was an order to the world. And I was born here. *(He indicates Philadelphia.)* I give you this brief summary of events, this overview, so you'll have some perspective. I'm sure I got some of it wrong, I've lost my notes, but it's basically the idea. And I wanted you to have, I think, some sense of history.

RAISED IN CAPTIVITY

Nicky Silver

Present, American City
Sebastian, 30s

Sebastian tells us about his parents.

SEBASTIAN. On Tuesday, my mother was taking a shower, when the shower-head, which was obviously loose to begin with, flew away from the wall and, propelled by water pressure, hit her in the head and killed her. Odd, as I knew her to be a person who, primarily took baths. I hadn't seen my mother in several years, although we spoke on the phone, on birthdays and Christmas. I left home when I was sixteen. I turned my back on everything and went off to pursue my education. My mother said, "Good luck," and my father said nothing, having died under mysterious circumstances before I was born. There were no pictures of him in our home and we never said his name. When asked about him, my mother abruptly changed the subject. Or, occasionally feigned sudden deafness. In any event, I walked away from servants and swimming pools to live on complimentary peanuts and cashews in cocktail lounges. My sister is watching me. From behind that tree.

REMEMBER THIS
Stephen Poliakoff

Present, England
Rick, 40s – 50s

Rick, alone onstage, stands facing the audience. He takes his shirt off and begins to describe his operation in great detail.

RICK. Plain sailing sounds distinctly ominous, I agree . . . but there is a surprise in store . . . Angiogram turns out to be a tube — stuck through your groin for some reason — and it weaves its way up to have a look . . .

Local anaesthetic . . . hence that sinister scraping sound you can hear . . . And that is exactly what it feels like to start with — a sense of them fiddling, scraping and entering you. And of course, since you're fully conscious, you can watch the whole thing if you want —

But I definitely didn't want to watch . . . Because the real surprise is . . . you get a gorgeous — yes, no other word for it — gorgeous floating sensation as the drugs kick in . . .

It turns into really great thinking time . . . ideas bombard you —

First guru thought . . . just a limbering-up one . . . the media soup is *literally* becoming a soup, in a way that nobody anticipated.

Everyone was so busy correcting their computers for a simple mechanical oversight, they missed the fact that our recent history was written on sand, and is being washed away . . .

I'm no Luddite . . . absolutely not, but second guru thought — it *is* genuinely thrilling to think of the things that are vanishing for ever — of which there will remain no trace at all. Each person will have a different list . . . But talk shows! — especially confessional talk shows — 'I slept with my wife's mother three times' — *Gone!* All celebrity chat will have vanished — and those endless real-life police videos of car chases that are on all the time — *Gone!* And comic amateur shots of old grannies' knickers falling down at wedding parties — *Gone! (Stares out.)* Isn't it fantastic to think that there might be no examples left — *not a single solitary one* — of any of that! *(He smiles.)* We have been recording everything and remembering nothing . . . ! Yes, *up to this moment* . . .

In the middle of the operation I begin to experiment in my head with a slightly new voice . . . with a media slur . . . the electronic dustman begins to transform . . . I have a definite sense of being cleaned for stardom . . .

People will look up the last period of the twentieth century and will have to tell what it was like from Hollywood movies . . . !

No letters to read either, because all those e-mails have gone . . .

So there will be no alternative except to try to remember . . .

The end of short-term memory . . . yes!

Even school kids may get interested in the recent past, because it is suddenly an endangered species . . .

It will become fashionable to remember . . . !

So I end the operation in a really good mood, despite the sinister scraping sound — it was great, I can recommend it.

And even better when I melt back into bed to recuperate, I find myself in the middle of quite incredible erotic thoughts . . .

SEA MARKS

Gardner McKay

Recent past, Ireland
Colm, 30s – 60s

Colm talks about his life.

COLM. I live by the sea.

I have always lived by the sea.

I can't know what it would be like living anywhere else.

The house I live in is made of stone that the sea has broken from these cliffs. It is a small house and stands close to the edge of the full tide. I am watching the sea now. It pushes up on the beach in front of the house. It is not a pretty beach. It is made of gray stones which the sea turns black by rising over them and falling away. The rain has stopped now and the sea is gray. The sky is white and lines of gray are being blown along further out at sea. There is always a gale somewhere on a day like this.

Each morning by the way the sea looks, I know how to feel. Its mood varies and so does mine. I can hear the sea, too, always. And I've seen every kind of fit it's able to throw against this shore. This shore. This shore is all the sea I know. The sea is a continent, and all I know of it are a few miles of this shore.

SEA MARKS

Gardner McKay

Recent past, Ireland
Colm, 30s – 60s

Colm talks about the sea.

COLM. I'll say a few words to you and then read you some marks that I made at a place as far away from this room as the other side of life. An island by the name of Cliffhorn Heads. In my language, the Irish, it would be called "Inish Shinderra." *(He pauses.)* Do any of you remember what a sunrise is like?

Sort of a gray meeting of the clouds at the east, and then a lightening of the sky, swiftening, lightening, swiftening, lightening until it is there?

Have any of you ever been out on the dark water, with not much sea running, and have known, really for true, that in a bit you'd be able to hold your hands out like this *(He holds his arms straight out at eye level, fingers stretched and raises them slightly.)* so that they could be warmed by the sun that is coming? For these elegances, you must become a fisherman. *(He pauses.)*

Fishing is, after all, a simple matter. You set your nets and you haul them in. You stay off the rocks at night and you anchor with care. And you look for signs that the sky is kind enough to provide. *(He pauses.)*

There are a number of people who do not understand the sea and I am among them. The sea is never simple — with its currents and strange habits — and bears watching. The sea is not a sentimental place to go — it is waiting for you to make a mistake. After all my years on it, I am kin to it, but I am not married to it — the sea is not a woman, after all.

THE SEAGULL

Anton Chekhov, translated by Dr. Carol Rocamora

Russia
Konstantin Gavrilovich Treplev, a young writer, 20s – 30s

TREPLEV. *(Preparing to write, reviews what he has already written.)*
Forms. For so long I've been going on and on about the need for new
forms. And now, little by little, I'm falling into the same old rut myself.
(Reads.) "The poster on the fence proclaimed it . . . a pale face, framed
by dark hair" . . . "proclaimed," "framed" . . . it's so trite. *(Crosses it out.)*
I'll start with the part where the hero is awakened by the sound of the
rain, and strike all the rest. All this about a moonlit night is drawn-out
and pretentious. Now Trigorin, he has technique, it's easy for him . . .
He's got a "broken bottle neck gleaming on the bank," a "mill wheel cast-
ing a somber shadow" — and presto — there's his moonlit night right
there. And what do I have — "the shimmering light," and "the soft twinkling of the stars," and "the distant sounds of the piano receding into the
quiet, fragrant air" . . . I mean, it's unbearable!

(Pause.)

Yes, more and more I've come to see . . . it's not about forms — old
forms, new forms — it's about writing, not bound by any forms at all,
just writing, freely, from the soul!

SEVEN YEAR ITCH
George Axelrod

1950s, New York
Richard, 20s – 30s

While waiting for the girl to arrive, Richard tries to justify his actions.

RICHARD. What am I *doing* anyway. This is absolutely ridiculous. The first night Helen leaves and I'm bringing dames into the apartment. Now take it easy. The girl upstairs almost kills me with a cast iron bucket. So I ask her down for a drink. What's wrong with that? If Helen was here, she'd do the same thing. It's only polite. And what is she doing asking Tom Mackenzie over for cocktails, if I may ask? Besides, I want to get another look at that girl. She must be some kind of a model or an actress or something. There is absolutely nothing wrong with asking a neighbor down for a drink. Nothing. I hope *she* doesn't get the wrong idea, that's all. If this dame thinks she's coming down here for some kind of a big time or something — well, she's in for a big surprise. One drink and out! That's all. I'm a happily married man, for Pete's sake! Maybe we ought to have a little soft music, just for atmosphere. Let's see. How about the 2nd Piano Concerto? Maybe Rachmaninoff would be overdoing it a little. This kid is probably more for old show tunes. . . . That's more like it. The old nostalgia. Never misses. . . . *Never misses?* What am I trying to do? I'll call her and tell her not to come. That's all. Why ask for trouble? I don't even know her phone number. I don't even know her name. What am I doing? And what the hell is *she* doing? She could have been down here, had her lousy drink, and gone home already. She's probably getting all fixed up. She'll probably be wearing some kind of evening dress! Oh, my God! What have I done? Well . . . you're in for it. If anything happens — it happens. That's all. It's up to her. She looked kind of sophisticated. She must know what she's doing. I'm pretty sophisticated myself. At least I used to be. I've been married so damn long I don't remember.

SEVEN YEAR ITCH

George Axelrod

1950s, New York
Richard, 20s – 30s

Richard tries to rationalize why the girl is still asleep in his bed.

RICHARD. There's not a thing in the world to worry about. Two very attractive, intelligent people happened to meet under circumstances that seemed to be . . . propitious . . . it happened. It was very charming and gay. In fact it was wonderful. But now it's over. We will just say goodbye like two intelligent people. We'll have coffee. . . . *(Knocks lightly twice, listens — opens door slightly — looks in — closes door, shudders.)* How can she possibly sleep like that! What's the matter with her anyway? Maybe she's sick or something. Maybe she's dead. Maybe the excitement was too much for her and she passed away in her sleep. Oh, my God! That means the police. And the reporters. "Actress found dead in publisher's apartment"! No. No. I'll just haul the body upstairs. That's all. Right back upstairs, nail up the floor again that's all. They'd have no reason to suspect me. I'd wear gloves of course. They'd never prove a thing. Oh, now stop it. You're getting hysterical again. Well, if she isn't dead, why the hell doesn't she just get up and go home! It's late! It's . . . late — it's really late — it's . . . *ten after eight?* It seemed later than *that* — Well, I'll give her another half hour to catch up on her beauty sleep. Then I'll very politely wake her. We'll have coffee like two intelligent people. And then I'll kiss her good-bye. It's been fun, darling, but now, of course, it's over . . . no tears — no regrets — Good-bye. It's been . . . swell.

SHADOWLANDS

William Nicholson

1950s, England
Lewis, 50s

Lewis talks to us about his friend.

LEWIS. Recently a friend of mine, a brave and Christian woman, collapsed in terrible pain. One minute she seemed fit and well. The next minute she was in agony. She is now in hospital, suffering from advanced bone cancer, and almost certainly dying. Why?

I find it hard to believe that God loves her. If you love someone, you don't want them to suffer. You can't bear it. You want to take their sufferings onto yourself. If even I feel like that, why doesn't God? Not just once in history, on the cross, but again and again? Today. Now.

It's at times like this that we have to remind ourselves of the very core of the Christian faith. There are other worlds than this. This world, that seems so real, is no more than a shadow of the life to come. If we believe that all is well in this present life, if we can imagine nothing more satisfactory than this present life, then we are under a dangerous illusion. All is not well. Believe me, all is not well.

SHADOWLANDS

William Nicholson

1950s, England
Lewis, 50s

Lewis expresses his feelings about God.

LEWIS. Good evening, the subject of my talk tonight is love, pain, and suffering.

Of course, as a comfortably situated middle-aged bachelor, I must be quite an authority on pain and love, wouldn't you have thought?

Now, by "pain" I don't mean a nagging discomfort in the intestines. For that matter, by "love" I don't mean a nagging discomfort in the intestines, either. The question I will put to you this evening, and one which I will attempt to answer, is this: If God loves us, why does He allow us to suffer so much? War. Pestilence. Famine.

(HE waves his newspaper at the audience.)

This is this morning's paper. Last night, as I'm sure you know, a number 1 bus drove into a column of young Royal Marine cadets in Chatham, and killed twenty-three of them. They were ten-year-old boys, marching and singing on their way to a boxing match. The road was unlit. The driver didn't see them. It was a terrible accident. Nobody was to blame. Except . . .

(HE points an accusing finger upwards.)

Now, where was He? Why didn't He stop it? What possible point can there be to such a tragedy? Isn't God supposed to be good? Isn't God supposed to love us?

Now, that's the nub of the matter: love. I think I'm right in saying that by "love," most of us mean either kindness or being "in love." But surely when we say that God loves us we don't mean that God is in love with us . . . do we? Not sitting by the telephone, writing letters: "I love you madly — God, xxx and hugs." At least I don't think so. Perhaps we mean that He's a kind God. Kindness is the desire to see others happy. Not happy in this way or that, but just happy.

SHYSTER
Brian Goluboff

Present, New York
Harry, 40s – 50s

In the darkness, Harry chants the Kaddish, the Jewish prayer for the dead. It's strangely beautiful. He stares at his father's Yahrzeit candle. He reaches into his wallet and takes out a dog-eyed piece of paper.

HARRY. Dear Rabbi Hirshkowitz, Parents, Relatives and Friends. On this, the day of my Bar Mitzvah, I wish to pay tribute to the great Jews of the past who fought so valiantly to keep our faith alive. From Moses parting the Red Sea and leading us to the Promised Land to Judah Maccabee and his brothers to David Ben Gurion fighting for our beloved Israel to my own great grandfather, Joseph, who battled the pogroms to keep the Sabbath and stowed away on a boat to give his family religious freedom in America — I wouldn't be here without this kind of bravery. I would also like to thank my own father, a pillar of this synagogue, who works as hard to teach his family the traditions of his faith as he does to put bread on the table. And on this, the dawn of my days as a Jewish man, the torch has been passed to me. I only hope that one day my own son will feel the same pride that I do now. Thank you.

SHYSTER
Brian Goluboff

Present, New York
Young Harry, 13

Young Harry addresses his friends and family at his Bar Mitzvah.

YOUNG HARRY. Rabbi Hirschkowitz, Dear Parents, Relatives and Friends . . . On this, the day of my Bar Mitzvah, I wish to pay tribute to the great Jews of the past who fought so valiantly to keep our faith alive. From Moses parting the Red Sea and leading our people to the Promised Land to Judah Maccabee and his brothers to David Ben Gurion fighting for our beloved Israel to my own great grandfather, Joseph, who battled the pogroms to keep the Sabbath and stowed away on a boat to give his family religious freedom in America — I wouldn't be here today without this kind of bravery. I would also like to thank, I would also like to thank . . . I would like to thank, uh . . . *(Harry steps away from the lectern, clears his throat, wipes the sweat from his forehead.)* I can't say this speech. It's a good speech that a lot of people helped me write, but it doesn't feel true, and I don't wanna stand up here and lie. I wanna tell you something from myself, you know . . . *(Pause.)* I wanted to quit this Bar Mitzvah because every time I walked to shul in my beanie, you know, my yarmulke, these kids on the street would kick my butt. But my father wouldn't let me quit, he kept making me go. At first it wasn't that big a deal, they'd hang me from the fence by my underwear, you know, give me a massive wedgie. Ha ha, no big deal, very funny. Then they started punching me their hardest right in the face. Then one of the kids cut me with a broken bottle. I hadda get stitches. I begged my father to let me stop going, but he wouldn't take no for an answer. So I'd get my butt beat on the street, then go in and learn how the Jews, since the beginning of time, it seems, got their butts beat around the world. At least I found out what we'd been chosen for . . . If it's true that "today I am a man," it is my belief that men make their own decisions. Well, this is my last day in shul. I don't wanna hurt anybody or disappoint anybody, but like I said, I don't wanna stand up here and B.S. you people . . . Doesn't mean we have to cancel the party. Let's eat and drink like chazzers, dance all night, drop your envelopes in the bag, but that's it for me, all right? I'm sorry . . .

SIDE MAN
Warren Leight

1980s, New York
Clifford, 20s – 30s

Clifford talks to the audience about his Dad.

CLIFFORD. When he's up there, blowing, he's totally in touch with everything that's going on around him. Ziggy bends a note, he echo's it instantly. A car horn sounds outside, he puts it into his solo, or harmonizes under it, a second later. I used to wonder how he could sense everything while he was blowing, and almost nothing when he wasn't. Now I just wonder how many more chances will I have to hear him blow. If I have kids . . . These guys are not even an endangered species any more. It's too late. There are no more big bands, no more territory bands. No more nonets, or tentets. No more sixty weeks a year on the road. No more jam sessions 'til dawn in the Cincinnati Zoo. When they go, that'll be it. No one will even understand what they were doing. A fifty year blip on the screen. Men who mastered their obsession, who ignored, or didn't even notice anything else. They played not for fame, and certainly not for money. They played for each other. To swing. To blow. Night after night, they were just burning brass. Oblivious.

SIX DEGREES OF SEPARATION

John Guare

1980s, New York
Paul, 20s – 30s

Paul tells us about his father.

PAUL. *(To us.)* Sidney Poitier, the future Jackie Robinson of films, was born the twenty-fourth of February, 1927 in Miami during a visit his parents made to Florida — legally? — to sell tomatoes they had grown on their farm in the Bahamas. He grew up on Cat Island, "so poor they didn't even own dirt" he has said. Neglected by his family, my father would sit on the shore, and, as he told me many times, "conjure up the kind of worlds that were on the other side and what I'd do in them." He arrived in New York City from the Bahamas in the winter of 1943 at age fifteen and a half and lived in the pay toilet of the bus station across from the old Madison Square Garden at Fiftieth and Eighth Avenue. He moved to the roof of the Brill building, commonly known as Tin Pan Alley. Washed dishes at the Turf restaurant for $4.11 a night. He taught himself to read by reading the newspaper. In the black newspaper, the theater page was opposite the want ad page. Among his 42 films are *No Way Out*, 1950 / *Cry the Beloved Country*, 1952 / *Blackboard Jungle*, 1955 / *The Defiant Ones*, 1958 / *Raisin in the Sun*, 1961 / *Lilies of the Field*, 1963 / *In the Heat of the Night*, 1967 / *To Sir With Love*, 1967 / *Shoot to Kill*, 1988 and, of course, *Guess Who's Coming To Dinner*. He won the Oscar for *Lilies of the Field* and was twice named top male box-office star in the country. My father made no films from 1977 to 1987 but worked as director and author. Dad said to me once, "I still don't fully understand how all that came about in the sequence it came about."

SNAKEBIT
David Marshall Grant

Present, Los Angeles
Michael, 20s – 30s

Everything is everywhere; stacks of books, pots from the kitchen, clothes, and a CD player. Michael, sits looking at the mess; after a while he speaks.

MICHAEL. I can't move. I'm not sleeping. Well, I sleep, but in fits and starts. I have dreams of anxiety: I can't find a place to live. I can't get the packing tape unstuck from the roll. They taught us in school moving is the most traumatic event you can go through. Second only to the loss of a loved one. I never understood that. I mean, really, don't you think, I don't know, kidnapping would be more traumatic than moving to Glendale? I had this client once who contracted polio three months before they came to his elementary school with the vaccine. He watched as his entire class was inoculated with tiny pinpricks of brand-new magic serum. Three months. How do you live with that? How do I live with that? They also taught us you should never get emotionally involved in work.

SOPHISTRY

Jonathan Marc Sherman

1990s, New England
Jack, 20s

*Jack tells the audience about when and why he went to see Whitey
on his own.*

JACK. This is how it happened. Thanksgiving break, most everybody
away from the campus, at home, visiting friends, anything to escape the
empty cold of this place during a vacation. Some stayed behind to do
work and some stayed behind . . . just because. I wasn't getting on well
with my folks then, I didn't want to go back home. I was tinkering
around with a sculpture project. It wasn't like I was just twiddling my
thumbs. I took Whitey's philosophy course that term. I wanted an extension on a paper. The paper wasn't late yet, I just thought I could do a
better job on it if I had a little extra time, another week or so. One night,
walking alone down the road, I saw the light in his apartment on. I headed
over there. He always told a bunch of us guys to stop by whenever we felt
like it, told us he'd give us stuff to eat and drink, whatever. Yeah, it was
weird, him being our teacher, but a few times we took him up on it, and
it was fine. He'd play music for us and give us beers and grill us sand-
wiches, fancy, not something simple like peanut butter. We'd always leave
early. It could get real depressing. Whitey would get this sad look in
his eyes, lonely, and he'd be soused, way drunk, which didn't help. But
Thanksgiving night, his light was on, and I figured it was a good idea to
ask for the extension. I mean, it was Thanksgiving, you know? I rang his
bell, and he came to the door, wearing pajama bottoms and an enormous
T-shirt. He'd been drinking, I could smell that, so I said maybe I should
come back another time.

A STATE AFFAIR

Robin Soans

Present, England
Paul, 20s – 30s

Paul talks about losing his friend.

PAUL. This one time Andy phones me . . . he's rattling, got no money, he says, 'Have you got any stuff?' I'd just had a dig — in my arse which is about the only place I've not been — and all I've got left is the wash — the residue left in the spoon — the shit basically. He says, 'That'll do, I'm coming round.' He hobbles in, puts his stick down, I sucked up the wash into a syringe, and I dig him in the neck. He starts going doolally, shouting all sorts, and hops out . . . out of his mind. I can't follow cos I've got this electronic tag on my leg. Twenty minutes later his mum phones. She's panicking, saying he's gone completely doolally, like he needs help urgently. I thought, 'Fuck it' — and ran out of the house. I found him outside the block of flats where he lived. He's thrown himself on to a metal fence. The spikes have gone through his chest. There's blood coming from his nose and ears. I have to physically lift him off. He's dead. This is my one and only best mate, and I've killed him. I told the police the first I knew was when his mum phoned for help.

A STATE AFFAIR

Robin Soans

Present, England
Peter, 20s – 30s

Peter gives us his schedule.

PETER. My diary for today.

Eight o'clock: Leave Fortress Tyrrell.

Eight-twenty: Meeting with the fire officer to discuss the introduction of the new weekly fire drill.

Eight-forty: Meeting with the two boys who've been climbing on the leisure centre roof. I know it's them, because we picked them up on the CCTV cameras last week, just before the cameras got nicked. I need to sort it out without going to the police . . . otherwise they get involved with the anti-social behaviour unit. If it goes down on record, the parents have to know; and, if repeated, the family can get evicted. All that needs to be avoided. A few sharp words from me should do.

Nine o'clock: Meeting with Lee van Cleef, aka Joyce Brett, to discuss the summer budgets.

Eleven o'clock: Meeting with the Resident's Association to sort out the car park. They can only have the cones out on a daily basis.

Eleven-thirty: Drive to Morrison's to buy prizes for bingo . . . storage jars, plastic beach balls, a pot plant, and a vanity case.

Twelve o'clock: Asda . . . food for bingo . . . buns, Coke, burgers, crisps, oven-ready chips.

Twelve forty-five: To the office to pick up messages, make calls, collect Grant's football boots which he left behind last week . . . stop his mother going on about them.

Two o'clock: Playscheme discussion with Mandy and Lorna . . . publicity . . . excellent publicity . . . I devised that myself . . . budget, dinner rota, consent forms, trip to Filey, bouncy castle, painting corner, cooking table, relay games, road safety . . . drop off shoeboxes for traffic lights . . . and I want to bring up Nicola for smoking dope on her way into the last playscheme.

Three o'clock: Meeting with Craig . . . it's a monitoring meeting . . . his suitability as a new playscheme assistant. He's a terrible shuffler. Will you stop shuffling, Craig. I'm not answering 'til you stop shuffling. And look me in the eye. I'll put him on a three-hour contract, and make it more when he stops shuffling.

Four o'clock: Meeting with Laura about the Pakistani girls outing. It turns out the male worker would be inappropriate for religious reasons.

Four-thirty: Back to centre, change, off to the gym for . . .

Four forty-five: Five-a-side football.

Six o'clock: Drive to Wibsey, via Buttershaw to drop off Grant's boots. Set up bingo. Legs eleven.

Six-thirty: Back to the office to do the accounts.

Eight-thirty: Clear up after bingo.

Nine o'clock: Home to Fortress Tyrrell.

TALLEY AND SON
Lanford Wilson

1940s, Missouri
Timmy, 20s

Addressing the audience, Timmy tells why he's here.

TIMMY. America won the Second World War today. It'll be August next year before anybody knows it, but we took Saipan, and from Saipan we'll take its little cousin island, Tinian, and from Tinian a B-29 can finally take off for Japan and get back again, and then the war's over. I'm a little early here. This is the Fourth of July; I'm due here on the sixth, for Granddad's funeral. I got my pass in my pocket. And while I'm here we're gonna have this big powwow about the family business. See, Harley Campbell and Dad own this garment factory, Talley and Son. Now some big company's wantin' to buy us out. Dad wrote me I'd better get my butt back here quick before Harley sold off everything but my stamp collection.

THREE DAYS OF RAIN

Richard Greenberg

1990s, New York
Walker, 30s

Walker introduces himself.

WALKER. Meanwhile, back in the city. . . . Two nights of insomnia. In this room, in the dark . . . listening . . . soaking up the Stravinsky of it. . . . No end to the sounds in a city. . . . Something happens somewhere, makes a noise, the noise travels, charts the distance: The Story of a Moment.

God, I need to sleep!

Yes. All right. Begin.

My name is Walker Janeway. I'm the son of Edmund Janeway, whose slightly premature death caused such a stir last year, I'm told.

As you're probably aware, my father, along with that tribe of acolytes who continue to people the firm of Wexler Janeway, designed all — yes, *all* — of the most famous buildings of the last thirty years. You've seen their pictures, you may have even visited a few. That Shi ite Mosque in Idaho. The new library in Bruges. The crafts museum in Austin, that hospice I forget where, and a vertical mall in Rhode Island that in square footage actually exceeds the *state* of Rhode Island.

Years and years and years ago, with his late partner, Theodore Wexler, my father also designed three or four buildings that truly *are* distinguished, chief among them: Janeway House.

I know you know that one.

Everyone's seen that one picture, *LIFE Magazine*, April of '63, I think, where it looks lunar, I mean, like something carved from the moon, mirage-y — you remember that photo? It's beautiful, isn't it? It won some kind of non-Pulitzer Prize that year. People have sometimes declined my invitation to see the real place for fear of ruining the experience of the photograph.

Well. The real place, as it happens, is a private home out in the desirable part of Long Island. My grandparents commissioned it of my father, using all the money they had in the world, because, I guess, they loved him so much. Apparently, there was something there for a parent to love. Hard to imagine how they could tell, though, since he seldom actually spoke. Maybe he was lovable in a Chaplinesque way.

Whatever, their faith paid off. The house is now deemed, by those who matter, to be one of the great private residences of the last half-century.

It's empty now.

My sister and I will inherit it today.

We'll be the only family present. Unless you count our friend, Pip, who is my late father's late partner's torpid son.

My mother would be, with us, too, of course, but she's, um, like, well, she's sort of like Zelda Fitzgerald's less stable sister, so she can't be there. She's elsewhere, she's . . .

So, then, this is the story as I know it so far:

My father was more-or-less silent; my mother was more-or-less mad. They married because by 1960 they had reached a certain age and they were the last ones left in the room.

And then they had my sister who is somehow *entirely* sane.

And then they had me.

And my father became spectacularly successful, and his partner died shockingly young, and my mother grew increasingly mad, and my sister and I were there so we had to grow up.

And today we receive our legacy.

THREE DAYS OF RAIN

Richard Greenberg

1990s, New York
Pip, 30s

Pip tells his story.

PIP. Hi. Hello. Okay: now me.

My name is Phillip O'Malley Wexler — well, Pip to those who've known me a little too long. My father, the architect Theodore Wexler, died of lung cancer at the age of thirty-eight, and even though he was the only one of his generation who never smoked. I was three when it happened, so, of course, I forgot him instantly. My mother tried to make up for this by obsessively telling me stories about him, this kind of rolling epic that trailed me through life, but they, or *it*, ended up being mostly about her. Which was probably for the best.

Anyway, it went like this:

My mother, Maureen O'Malley back then, came to New York in the spring of '59. She was twenty, her parents staked her to a year, and she arrived with a carefully-thought-out plan to be amazing at something. Well, the year went by without much happening and she was miserable because she was afraid she was going to have to leave New York and return, in disgrace, to Brooklyn.

Early one morning, after a night when she couldn't sleep at all, she started wandering around the city. It was raining, she had her umbrella, she sat in the rain under her umbrella on a bench in Washington Square Park, and felt sorry for herself. Then she saw my father for the first time.

"There he was," she told me, "this devastatingly handsome man" — that was an exaggeration, he looked like me — and he was obviously, miraculously, even *more* unhappy than she was. He was just thrashing through the rain, pacing and thrashing, until, all at once, he stopped and sank onto the bench beside her. But not because of her. He didn't realize she was there. He didn't have an umbrella so my mother shifted hers over to him.

"Despair," my mother told me, "can be attractive in a young person. Despair in a young person can be seductive."

Well, eventually she got tired of him not noticing the wonderful thing she was doing for him so she said, a little too loudly: "Can I help you? May I be of help to you?"

Because he'd been crying.

And he jumped! Man, he *shrieked!*

But he stayed anyway, and they talked, and I was born, the end.

Okay. So, my mother had been telling me that story for about ten years before it occurred to me to ask: "Why was he crying? What was my father so upset about the first time he met you?" "I never knew," she said. He just told her he was fine, she took him to breakfast, they talked about nothing, and I guess she kind of gawked at him. And the more she gawked, I guess the happier he felt, because by the end of the breakfast it was as if nothing had happened and they were laughing and my mother was in love and the worst day of her life had become the best day of her life.

When she first came to New York, my mother would stay up till dawn debating Abstract Expressionism and *Krapp's Last Tape*, and then she'd sneak out to a matinee of one of those plays you could never remember the plot of where the girl got caught in the rain and had to put on the man's bathrobe and they sort of did a little dance around each other and fell in love. And there wasn't even a single good joke, but my mother would walk out after and the city seemed dizzy with this absolutely random happiness, and that's how she met my father.

She's hardly ever home anymore. She travels from city to city.

I think she's looking for another park bench, and another wet guy. That's okay. I hope she finds him.

TITUS ANDRONICUS

William Shakespeare

Aaron, 40s – 50s

Aaron talks about his plans to sweep Tamora off her feet.

AARON. Now climbeth Tamora Olympus' top,
    Safe out of fortune's shot; and sits aloft,
    Secure of thunder's crack or lightning's flash;
    Advanc'd above pale envy's threatening reach.
    As when the golden sun salutes the morn,
    And, having gilt the ocean with his beams,
    Gallops the zodiac in his glistening coach,
    And overlooks the highest-peering hill;
    So Tamora:
    Upon her will doth earthly honour wait,
    And virtue stoops and trembles at her frown.
    Then, Aaron, arm thy heart and fit thy thoughts
    To mount aloft with thy imperial mistress,
    And mount her pitch, whom thou in triumph long
    Hast prisoner held, fetter'd in amorous chains,
    And faster bound to Aaron's charming eyes
    Than is Prometheus tied to Caucasus.
    Away with slavish weeds and servile thoughts!
    I will be bright, and shine in pearl and gold,
    To wait upon this new-made empress.
    To wait, said I? to wanton with this queen,
    This goddess, this Semiramis, this nymph,
    This syren, that will charm Rome's Saturnine,
    And see his shipwreck and his common-weal's. —
    Holla! what storm is this?

TORCH SONG TRILOGY

Harvey Fierstein

1970s, New York
Arnold, 20s – 30s

Arnold calls Murray on the phone, leaves a message then waits. Finally, it rings and Murray gets told off.

ARNOLD. "Having completed the hexagram, compare it to the chart on page 228." Here it is. Number thirty-eight. Here we go. "Hexagram Thirty-eight. Koo-eeeoiiiii. The Estranged."

Hello, Murray? Call me back.

Goddammit, Murray, what took you so long? . . . The shower could have waited Murray. . . . The shampoo in the shower could have waited, Murray. . . . The man with the shampoo in the shower could have waited, Murray. Anyway, I can't talk now. I gotta keep the line free. What? . . . I just wanted to make sure the phone was working. . . . Ed. Alright? I'm expecting a call from Ed. . . . When? Well, it is now Tuesday, eight P.M. Well, Ed's gonna call sometime after Tuesday eight P.M. . . . Of course he's gonna call, Murray. You think I'd sit by the phone for six days if he wasn't gonna call? . . . You are getting on my nerves, Murray. Look he is a very busy man. With a great many responsibilities. He will call me when he is able. And I will understand. Got it! When you have been seeing someone for four months, Murray, you build a relationship based on trust and mutual respect. Something you and your Magic fingers shower massage would not understand. He will call, Murray. He knows when he's got a good thing going. He knows I ain't like those other cheap tricks he sees. He knows I got something that puts me above those runned up the mill, always on Sunday, anyplace I hang my crotch is home variety of homosexual commonly cruised in these here parts. I am important, Murray. I am impressive, Murray. But most of all, Murray, I am mysterious. Which is a quality you don't find on every bar stool. Oh, no, Murray, he will call. And when he does. . . . And when he does. . . . And when he does. . . . The phone's gonna be free! *(slams down the phone, pouting)* Oh ye of little faith!

THE TRIUMPH OF LOVE

Pierre Marivaux, translated by Stephen Wadsworth

Ancient Greece
Harlequin, any age

*Harlequin is discovered in a pose of despair, crying noisily. He plays the
scene with many changes of voice, gesturing wildly and moving suddenly
from one part of the stage to another.*

HARLEQUIN: Ah, unhappy me! Will I ever be able to marry Corine?
The situation is rich with misery. First of all, does she even love me? I
would think that . . . to look at me is to love me, and when she *is* looking at me I am sure that she does love me; it's only when she stops looking at me that I'm not sure she does anymore, or ever did really. And even
if she did, or does, or always will, she can't just *have* me, as she is a lady's
maid, a servant, one of her mistress' belongings, who has as many rights
as her petticoat. But I err! For her petticoat can do precisely what she
cannot — rise! *(He laughs.)* And though I am but a servant and have no
rights, I have only to think of her, and I can do what she cannot — rise!
(More laughter.) And I cannot just have *her*, either, because not only do I
serve, but I serve Hermocrate, and the chances of his allowing me to leave
his service to pursue *love* . . . grow slimmer with every panting breast . . .
uh, *passing breath!* Ah, how shall I be able to live without Corine? I would
rather die first. *(A beat.) Die?!* Die! That's it. Let me see . . . some unusual
sort of death. An heroic death, a *horrible* death . . . a *hanging* death!
That's it! *(Racing frantically about, miming the actions he describes.)* I shall
go to my room, tie a chair to a crossbeam, climb upon a rope, place the
chair around my neck, kick away the chair . . . *(Cheerfully.)* . . . and I'm
hanged! I'll hang now, then elope, and then when I'm arrested for the
crime of escaping my master I'll not have to hang again, because who
would hang a man who's already been hanged?! It's perfect!

TRUST
Steven Dietz

Present, American City
Roy, 30s

Roy swigs from a beer, then addresses the audience.

ROY. Damn.

The simplest things are the hardest to recreate.

There. Now, *that's* wisdom. And, as we know, wisdom and a buck'll get you coffee-to-go. Beyond that?

Women?

I get nervous about women.

And when I get nervous, I do two things:

I drink any beer but Coors.

And I steal.

Not big things.

Pocket things. *(He pulls a large bag of M&M's out of his coat and tosses it into the laundry basket.)*

Title: I was nervous today.

I was at my regular cafe for lunch, Caesar salad and a Butterfinger malt, and there are two women talking at the table next to me. Their faces were a *foot apart* man. *(He holds the palms of his hands four inches apart.)*

They actually *talked like that* for an *hour.* I mean, do they really expect us to be able to do that? Two men could not lean across a table and do that. If two men tried to do that, everyone would assume they were plotting a murder and they would be arrested. But, there they were — *(Holds up his hands again, as before.) talking.* And this is what they're saying: "Well, for my part, I've sworn them off until I meet a man who really understands how a woman thinks." *(Pause. He takes a restaurant napkin dispenser from his coat and tosses it in the basket.)*

Great. There is nothing quite like having your greatest fear confirmed. You feel strangely at peace. At peace in the way a, say, *cold corpse in a coffin* must feel at peace. I wanted to say something to them. I wanted to, you know, plead my — our — case, but there was no getting in. They were — *(Holds his hands up, as before.)* — *you* know.

Okay, I thought. I will combat this. I understand some things. I will think about the things that I *do* understand and determine whether I can make a fulfilling personal life out of them. I understand these things: the game of Yahtzee, most comic strips, the appeal of Thai cuisine, Bukowski's poetry, Dylan's songs, and, of course, Spin Art. Looking at this list, I think I'll be spending a lot of Saturday nights at the laundromat with a crossword puzzle. I don't know.

TWELFTH NIGHT
William Shakespeare

Malvolio, 40s – 50s

A smitten Malvolio talks about the love letter he has just received.

MALVOLIO. Oh, ho! do you come near me now? no worse man than Sir Toby to look to me? This concurs directly with the letter: she sends him on purpose that I may appear stubborn to him; for she incites me to that in the letter. *Cast thy humble slough,* says she; — *be opposite with a kinsman, surly with servants, — let thy tongue tang with arguments of state, — put thyself into the trick of singularity;* — and, consequently, sets down the manner how; as, a sad face, a reverend carriage, a slow tongue, in the habit of some sir of note, and so forth. I have limed her; but it is Jove's doing, and Jove make me thankful! And, when she went away now, *Let this fellow be looked to:* Fellow! not Malvolio, nor after my degree, but fellow. Why, everything adheres together; that no dram of a scruple, no scruple of a scruple, no obstacle, no incredulous or unsafe circumstance, — What can be said? Nothing, that can be, can come between me and the full prospect of my hopes. Well, Jove, not I, is the doer of this, and he is to be thanked.

VISITING MR. GREEN
Jeff Baron

1990s, New York
Ross, 20s – 30s

Ross stops by for his weekly visit with Mr. Green, the man he ran over.

ROSS. *(Calls out toward the bedroom.)* Hi, Mr. Green. It's Ross. I'm here. You're thrilled, I know. My lawyer and my city councilwoman both called the judge. He's not gonna change his mind. There's mail in your mailbox. We could wait until it explodes again, or you could just give me the key and I'll go down and get it. Though I see you're still savoring last weeks mail. *(A beat.)* I don't see a clock in here. I can bring you one. So you'll know when to expect me. I'll be here every Thursday, seven o'clock sharp. That's gonna be a lot easier, now that I've told my boss about you. *(A beat.)* I didn't actually mention the accident. I don't want to be known around the company for mowing down eighty-six-year-olds. I just told him I'm doing some volunteer work. Come on, Mr. Green. Don't let your soup get cold.

WAITING ROOM

Lisa Loomer

Present, New York
Larry, 40s

Larry talks to his wife on the phone.

LARRY. Uh-hunh. . . . Uh-huh. . . . Well, I hear what you're saying, sweetie, and I can certainly empathize with — . . . Well, I don't think it's necessary to reiterate what you. . . . Ca — I think what Jeff meant when he said we should "mirror each other's feelings" was that we — . . . No, not that we reiterate — hold on a sec, sweetie — *(Loudly, to an imaginary interruption.)* Yes? Did you want something, Phyllis? I'm talking to my wife. Sorry, sweetie — *(To "Phyllis.")* Well, then the board will just have to wait, Phyllis. Just tell the board that I am speaking with my wife and they will have to wait. So who's this new doctor you want to go see? . . . Deepak Chopper? . . . What's his theory? Three kinds of body types, kapha, vatta, pitta. . . . You're a kapha, I'm a what? . . . A pitta? . . . I'm not a pitta, Cathy . . . I'm not a pitta. Because it sounds like "pitiful"!

A WARWICKSHIRE TESTIMONY

April De Angelis

1960s, England
Diggie, 20s – 30s

Diggie alone in the woods.

DIGGIE. I sleep in this wood sometimes. I sleep where I can. I like the smell of earth. I clear weeds away sometimes but nobody can see. They come back quick enough, but I like the work. In the other place I didn't like it. The bodies came too fast. Swinging towards you another and another. Stab, slit. Stab, slit. Then another. Swinging away, swing towards you. Your feet in the blood. The stink. Pigs screaming, machines shrilling. In twenty seconds they've bled to death. You know what's coming towards you; a death and another and another and your heart shuts off. That's your bit of peace. It's peaceful here. Except when he comes. I don't like to see him. I don't like to see him with the girl. He has her by the arm and he pulls her. She is talking to him all the while but he's not listening. She's a pretty girl. I found an orchid here that's very rare. You don't see them much. Like a single white flame balancing on its stalk. Things have gone. Things you saw every day. Flowers. Primroses. They used to be everywhere. Birds have gone too. It's quieter in the woods. Maybe they all flew away one winter and decided not to come back. I might have done that if I was a bird. She's saying to him to let her go. But he's not. She's white. Her face is white and her hair is stuck to it dark like weeds. He has her by the arm and he's not letting go. He has a coat on like a soldier's so it's harder to make him out, but her white face sticks out. There she is. There's the orchid. She's still there. I could watch her all day. White lady we used to call her. Nobody comes here. Nobody should hurt you. Army green. I can see him now. She fights him but he has a knife. Please stop. Please. Then it gets dark. All the while the white lady glows in the dark like a flame. By her it's peaceful.

WAVERLY GALLERY

Kenneth Lonnergan

1990s, New York
Daniel, 20s

*Daniel tells the audience about the situation with the gallery
and his mother.*

DANIEL. I did go to see Mr. George. I asked him for another year. Just one more year before he took away the gallery, because after that it wouldn't make any difference anymore. And I thought it would make a great difference now.

He was very sympathetic. He said he had an aunt who was going through the same thing. But he told me the same thing he told my mother on the phone. The cafe was scheduled to open *that* summer, and there was absolutely nothing he could do about it.

Then he asked if we'd given any thought to putting Gladys in a home. I got kind of angry and I said we didn't really want to do that. She didn't like old people. She liked to be where the action was. She thought she was running a gallery. He said this is really the time her family should be taking care of her. *(Pause.)* There were no more attempts to dissuade him.

I kept thinking there must be something we could do, only I just couldn't think of what it was. I had a dream where I put her on a bus from Vermont to New York, and I wanted to get her settled and get off, but as she hobbled down the aisle I was afraid she'd be knocked over by the bus's motion, and it occurred to me that she'd never know where to change buses, that it was impossible to put her on a bus by herself because she'd never make it. But I couldn't go with her and was all too late. Her mind was smashed to pieces, and the person she used to be hadn't really been around for a long time. . . . But the pieces were still *her* pieces. *(Pause.)* I guess we all wanted to get out of it.

WHERE HAS TOMMY FLOWERS GONE?

Terrence McNally

Present, New York City
Tommy, 20s – 30s

Tommy talks about the woman he just met.

TOMMY. Her name's Greta Prince and I'm crazy about her legs. I've had my eye on her since they called the flight. So far I'm batting zero but I've still got about another hour and a half. You see, I don't know where I'm going to sleep when I get back to the Big Apple tonight. I thought I was on my way home today but I decided not to go after all. Home means St. Petersburg, Florida. It's famous for green benches, orange Rexall drugstores, pale old people and death. I love it. I just wanted to make sure everyone back home was all right, you know? I mean I didn't particularly want to talk to anyone, just see them again. Well, maybe next time. You know what America looks like at one in the morning from 33,000 feet? A big dark place with a couple of tiny twinkling lights. It's so empty down there! No doubt about it, flying gets you very philosophical. So does looking at America from 33,000 feet. At ground level you just get either very scared or very depressed.

WHERE HAS TOMMY FLOWERS GONE?

Terrence McNally

Present, New York City
Arnold, any age

Arnold tells us his story.

ARNOLD. I didn't always have Tommy Flowers and I'm not at all sure I always will. I got him when I was given back to him by a friend of his who didn't want me after Tommy had given me to him in the first place. It's complicated, I know. This friend was a very lonely sort of person and Tommy decided that he should have a dog. Only he didn't want a dog. But when he saw me something inside of him must have snapped because his eyes kind of filled up like he was going to cry and he held me very close. I was this big then! And he didn't say anything and he walked a few feet away from everyone and stood with his back to them and just held me like a little baby. No one had to ask if he wanted me. You could just tell. I was so happy. But the next morning he didn't want me at all. There I was, just kind of slumped in my box, all droopy-eyed and warm-nosed and not looking at all too hot. Puppy chill is all it was. Tommy said they'd just take me to the vet but the friend didn't want a sick dog. He didn't want any dog. And you know what his reason was? They die on you. That's what he said. They die on you. We do, you know. Everything does. But is that a reason? How could anyone not want me? Oh, don't get any ideas. I'm not a talking dog. I'm a thinking one. There's a difference!

WHERE HAS TOMMY FLOWERS GONE?

Terrence McNally

Present, New York City
Tommy, 20s – 30s

*Tommy addresses the audience and tells them all the people he wants to
dedicate the act to.*

TOMMY. I would like to thank the following people for making me
what I am today:

Mom and Dad; my big brother Harry; my wonderful Nana; my
beloved Grandpa; Walt Disney; The Little Engine That Could; Golden
Books; American nuns; Batman and Robin and all the gang over at Dell
Comics; Little Lulu; Wonder Woman; Betty and Jughead; Rossini, the
Lone Ranger and Tonto, too; Cream of Wheat for Let's Pretend; all
MGM musicals but especially the one with Abba Dabba Honeymoon;
Ringling Brothers, Barnum and Bailey; Francis the Talking Mule; Ma
and Pa Kettle and their farm; B.O. Plenty and Sparkle; Henry Aldrich in
the Haunted House; Abbott and Costello; the Wolf Man; Kukla, Fran
and Ollie; Uncle Miltie and my real Uncle Fred; Harry S. Truman; Mar-
garet S. Truman; Gene Autry and his girdle (if he ever really wore one);
Roy Rogers and Dale Evans; Johnny Weismuller; Johnny Sheffield, Sabu;
Esther Williams; Joe DiMaggio; Pee Wee Reese; Jackie Robinson; Ralph
Bunche; Trygve Lie; Miss America; Mr. America; the Weavers; Patty
Page; Babe Diedrickson Zaharias; Mme. Chiang Kai-shek; Chuck Berry;
the Coasters; Candy Barr; Lili St. Cyr; all strippers who worked with an-
imals but especially snakes; Ava Gardner; Hal Wallis; Corinne Calvet;
Jerry Lee Lewis and plain Jerry Lewis; Johnny Mathis; Terry Moore; ol'
Marilyn up there, of course; James Dean; Elvis Presley; John F. Kennedy;
Rose F. Kennedy; Fidel Castro; Bernadette Castro (hell, why not?); Che
Guevara; Bob Dylan; Ho Chi Minh; the Beatles; Miss Teenage America;
Mme. Nhu; Lady Bird Johnson; Lyndon Bird Johnson; Lynda Bird

Johnson Robb; Luci Bird Johnson Nugent; the Rolling Stones; Janis Joplin; the Man From Glad; Richard M. Nixon; the last girl I balled and all the sisters of mercy to come *and* . . . whew! . . . we really do get by with a little help from our friends . . . Mr. Thomas Jefferson, who said something about God forbid we should ever be twenty years without a rebellion! To all of them I dedicate this act. Oh, yeah, I'm Tommy Flowers. Hi.

ZERO POSITIVE

Harry Kondoleon

1980s, New York
Patrick, 20s – 30s

Patrick enters as a soldier and speaks.

PATRICK. I am the herald, sad messenger of the gods too weary to
                make of my job lightness,
    I arrive at dawn with heavy news of a world crashing down.
    I stand before it, the ruins of Athens.
    Woe to all things.
    Woe to us witnesses as the sun rises.
    We witness the waste of all things' power.
    Woe to me, sad herald, witness to the pestilence of the city —
    A city that during holy season could not be polluted by
                public executions
    Lies now an open grave.
    Every misery that can befall a city falls here.
    It is a deep and narrow grave:
    Scorching in heat, freezing by night.
    Hunger and Thirst.
    The corpses of those who died
    Lie with those that follow.
    Fleet and army perished, few return home.
    O Muse, help me to finish.
    The words stick in my mouth, sad soldiers.
    Messengers of the gods, take back your prophecies.
    They say the war is over.
    But in the vanquished city
    Defeat and ruin battle still for title
    As morning makes its mark
    Upon the dug-deep scars of Fate.

PERMISSIONS

AFTER THE FALL Copyright 1964 by Arthur Miller. Reprinted by Permission of International Creative Management. Contact: ICM 40 West 57th Street, New York, NY 10019.

AH, WILDERNESS Copyright 1960 by Eugene O'Neill. Reprinted by Permission of the William Morris Agency. Contact: William Morris Agency, 1325 Avenue of the Americas, New York, NY 10019, attn: Samuel Liff.

ALKÊSTIS Copyright 2003 translated by Carl R. Mueller. Reprinted by Permission of the Author. Contact: Smith and Kraus Publishers, P.O. Box 127, Lyme, NH 03768.

AMPHITRYON Copyright 1995 translated by Richard Wilbur. Reprinted by Permission of William Morris Agency, Inc. on behalf of the Author. CAUTION: Professionals and amateurs are hereby warned that "AMPHITRYON" is subject to a royalty. It is fully protected under the copyright laws of the United States of America, and of all countries covered by the International Copyright Union (including the Dominion of Canada and the rest of the British Commonwealth), and of all countries covered by the Pan-American Copyright Convention and the Universal Copyright Convention, the Berne Convention and of all countries with which the United States has reciprocal copyright relations. All rights, including professional/ amateur stage rights, motion picture, recitation, lecturing, public reading, radio broadcasting, television, video or sound recording and all other forms of mechanical or electronic reproduction, such as CD-ROM, CD-I, information storage and retrieval systems and photocopying, and the rights of translation into foreign languages, are strictly reserved. Particular emphasis is placed upon the matter of readings, permission for which must be secured from the Author's agent in writing. Inquiries concerning rights should be addressed to William Morris Agency, Inc., 1325 Avenue of the Americas, New York, NY 10019, attn: Peter Franklin.

ANDROMACHE Copyright 1982 translated by Richard Wilbur. Reprinted by Permission of William Morris Agency, Inc. on behalf of the Author. CAUTION: Professionals and amateurs are hereby warned that "ANDROMACHE" is subject to a royalty. It is fully protected under the copyright laws of the United States of America, and of all countries covered by the International Copyright Union (including the Dominion of Canada and the rest of the British Commonwealth), and of all countries covered by the Pan-American Copyright Convention and the Universal Copyright Convention, the Berne Convention and of all countries with which the United States has reciprocal copyright relations. All rights, including professional/ amateur stage rights, motion picture, recitation, lecturing, public reading, radio broadcasting, television, video or sound recording and all other forms of mechanical or electronic reproduction, such as CD-ROM, CD-I, information storage and retrieval systems and photocopying, and the rights of translation into foreign languages, are strictly reserved. Particular emphasis is placed upon the matter of readings, permission for which must be secured from the Author's agent in writing. Inquiries concerning rights should be addressed to William Morris Agency, Inc., 1325 Avenue of the Americas, New York, NY 10019, attn: Peter Franklin.

ANNE OF THE THOUSAND DAYS Copyright 1948 by Maxwell Anderson. Reprinted by Permission of Anderson House Publishers. Contact: Robert A. Freedman Dramatic Agency, Inc., 1501 Broadway, Suite 2310, New York, NY 10036.

ART Copyright 1994 by Yasmina Reza, trans. by Christopher Hampton, 1996. Reprinted by permission of Faber and Faber Ltd. Contact: Faber and Faber Limited, 3 Queen Square, London WC1N 3AU, England.

AVOW Copyright 2000 by Bill C. Davis. Reprinted by Permission of the Author. Contact: Renaissance/AMG, 140 West 57th Street, Suite 2A, New York, NY 10019.

THE BAKKHAI Copyright 2003 translated by Carl Mueller. Reprinted by Permission of the Author. Contact: Smith and Kraus Publishers, P.O. Box 127, Lyme, NH 03768.

THE BOYS NEXT DOOR Copyright 1988 by Tom Griffin. Reprinted by Permission of William Morris Agency, Inc. on behalf of the Author. CAUTION: Professionals and amateurs are hereby warned that "THE BOYS NEXT DOOR" is subject to a royalty. It is fully protected under the copyright laws of the United States of America, and of all countries covered by the International Copyright Union (including the Dominion of Canada and the rest of the British Commonwealth), and of all countries covered by the Pan-American Copyright Convention and the Universal Copyright Convention, the Berne Convention and of all countries with which the United States has reciprocal copyright relations. All rights, including professional/ amateur stage rights, motion picture, recitation, lecturing, public reading, radio broadcasting, television, video or sound recording and all other forms of mechanical or electronic reproduction, such as CD-ROM, CD-I, information storage and retrieval systems and photocopying, and the rights of translation into foreign languages, are strictly reserved. Particular emphasis is placed upon the matter of readings, permission for which must be secured from the Author's agent in writing. Inquiries concerning rights should be addressed to William Morris Agency, Inc., 1325 Avenue of the Americas, New York, NY 10019, attn: Steve Spiegel.

THE BUNGLER Copyright 2000 translated by Richard Wilbur. Reprinted by Permission of Peter Franklin. Reprinted by Permission of Dramatists Play Service, Inc. CAUTION: The excerpt from THE BUNGLER included in this volume is reprinted by permission of Dramatists Play Service, Inc. The English language stock and amateur stage performance rights in this Play are controlled exclusively by Dramatists Play Service, 440 Park Avenue South, New York, NY 10016. No professional or nonprofessional performance of the Play may be given without obtaining, in advance, the written permission of Dramatists Play Service, Inc., and paying the requisite fee. Inquiries concerning all other rights should be addressed to Dramatists Play Service, 440 Park Avenue South, New York, NY 10016.

THE CHOSEN Copyright 2000 by Aaron Posner & Chaim Potok. Reprinted by Permission of the Authors. Reprinted by Permission of Mary Harden a/a/f the Author. CAUTION: Professionals and amateurs are hereby warned that performance of THE CHOSEN is subject to a royalty. It is fully protected under the copyright laws of the United States of America, and of all countries covered by the International Copyright

Union (including the Dominion of Canada and the rest of the British Commonwealth), and of all countries covered by the Pan-American Copyright Convention and the Universal Copyright Convention, the Berne Convention and of all countries with which the United States has reciprocal copyright relations. All rights, including professional/ amateur stage rights, motion picture, recitation, lecturing, public reading, radio broadcasting, television, video or sound recording and all other forms of mechanical or electronic reproduction, such as CD-ROM, CD-I, information storage and retrieval systems and photocopying, and the rights of translation into foreign languages, are strictly reserved. Particular emphasis is placed upon the matter of readings, permission for which must be secured from the Author's agent in writing. Inquiries concerning all other rights should be addressed to Mary Harden, Harden-Curtis Associates, 850 Seventh Avenue, Suite 405, New York, NY 10019.

CIDER HOUSE RULES, PART ONE Copyright 2001 by Peter Parnell. Reprinted by Permission of Helen Merrill Agency on behalf of the Author. Contact: Helen Merrill Ltd. a/a/f Parnell, attn: Beth Blickers, 295 Lafayette St., Ste. 915, New York, NY 10012-2700.

CONVERSATIONS AFTER A BURIAL Copyright 2000 by Yasmina Reza. Reprinted by Permission of Faber and Faber. Contact: Faber and Faber, 3 Queen Square, London, WC1N 3AU.

CYCLOPS Copyright 2003 translated by Carl R. Mueller. Reprinted by Permission of the Author. Contact: Smith and Kraus Publishers, P.O. Box 127, Lyme, NH 03768.

DANCING AT LUGHNASA Copyright 1968 by Brian Friel. Reprinted by Permission of Faber and Faber. Contact: Faber and Faber, 3 Queen Square, London, WC1N 3AU.

THE DEATH OF BESSIE SMITH Copyright 1959, 1960, 1987, 1988 by Edward Albee. Reprinted by Permission of William Morris Agency, Inc. on behalf of the Author. CAUTION: Professionals and amateurs are hereby warned that "THE DEATH OF BESSIE SMITH" is subject to a royalty. It is fully protected under the copyright laws of the United States of America, and of all countries covered by the International Copyright Union (including the Dominion of Canada and the rest of the British Commonwealth), and of all countries covered by the Pan-American Copyright Convention and the Universal Copyright Convention, the Berne Convention and of all countries with which the United States has reciprocal copyright relations. All rights, including professional/amateur stage rights, motion picture, recitation, lecturing, public reading, radio broadcasting, television, video or sound recording and all other forms of mechanical or electronic reproduction, such as CD-ROM, CD-I, information storage and retrieval systems and photocopying, and the rights of translation into foreign languages, are strictly reserved. Particular emphasis is placed upon the matter of readings, permission for which must be secured from the Author's agent in writing. Inquiries concerning rights should be addressed to William Morris Agency, Inc., 1325 Avenue of the Americas, New York, NY 10019, attn: Owen Laster.

DEFYING GRAVITY Copyright 1998 by Jane Anderson. Reprinted by Permission of the Author. Contact: The Gage Group, 14724 Ventura Blvd., #505, Sherman Oaks, CA 91403, attn: Martin Gage.

THE GOODBYE PEOPLE Copyright 1974 by Herb Gardner. Reprinted by Permission of International Creative Management, Inc. Contact: International Creative Management, Inc., 40 West 57th Street, New York, NY 10019, attn: Katharine Cluverius.

HARVEY Copyright 1944, 1971 by Mary Chase. Reprinted by Permission of Robert A. Freedman Dramatic Agency, Inc. CAUTION: Professionals and amateurs are hereby warned that performance of HARVEY is subject to payment of a royalty. It is fully protected under the copyright laws of the United States of America, and of all countries covered by the International Copyright Union (including the Dominion of Canada and the rest of the British Commonwealth), and of all countries covered by the Pan-American Copyright Convention, the Universal Copyright Convention, the Berne Convention, and of all countries with which the United States has reciprocal copyright relations. All rights, including professional/amateur stage rights, motion picture, recitation, lecturing, public reading, radio broadcasting, television, video or sound recording, and all other forms of mechanical or electronic reproduction, such as CD-ROM, CD-I, DVD, information storage and retrieval systems and photocopying, and the rights of translation into foreign languages, are strictly reserved. Particular emphasis is placed upon the matter of readings, permission for which must be secured from the Author's agent in writing. The nonprofessional stage performance rights in HARVEY are controlled exclusively by DRAMATISTS PLAY SERVICE, INC., 440 Park Avenue South, New York, NY 10016. No nonprofessional performance of the Play may be given without obtaining in advance the written permission of DRAMATISTS PLAY SERVICE, INC. and paying the requisite fee. Inquiries concerning all other rights should be addressed to Robert A. Freedman Dramatic Agency, Inc., 1501 Broadway, Suite 2310, New York, NY 10036. SPECIAL NOTE: Anyone receiving permission to produce HARVEY is required to give credit to the Author as sole and exclusive Author of the Play on the title page of all programs distributed in connection with performances of the Play and in all instances in which the title of the Play appears for purposes of advertising, publicizing, or otherwise exploiting the Play and/or a production thereof. The name of the Author must appear on a separate line, in which no other name appears, immediately beneath the title and in size of type equal to 50% of the size of the largest, most prominent letter used for the title of the Play. No person, firm or entity may receive credit larger or more prominent than that accorded the Author.

HEAVEN Copyright 2000 by George Walker. Reprinted by Permission of Talon Books, Ltd. of Canada. Contact: Great North Artists Management, 350 Dupont Street, Toronto, Ontario, Canada M5R 1V9.

THE HOLOGRAM THEORY Copyright 2000, 2001 by Jessica Goldberg. Reprinted by Permission of the Author. CAUTION: Professionals and amateurs are hereby warned that THE HOLOGRAM THEORY is subject to a royalty. It is fully protected under the copyright laws of the United States of America, and of all countries covered by the International Copyright Union (including the Dominion of Canada and the rest of the British Commonwealth), and of all countries covered by the Pan-American Copyright Convention and the Universal Copyright Convention, and of all countries with which

138

Convention, and of all countries with which the United States has reciprocal copyright relations. All rights, including professional, amateur, motion picture, recitation, lecturing, public reading, radio broadcasting, television, video or sound taping, all other forms of mechanical or electronic reproductions such as information storage and retrieval systems and photocopying, and all rights of translation into foreign languages, are strictly reserved. Particular emphasis is laid upon the question of readings, permission for which must be secured from the Author's agent in writing. Inquiries concerning stock and amateur performance rights should be addressed to Dramatic Publishing, P.O. Box 129, Woodstock, IL 60098-0129. Inquiries concerning all other rights should be addressed to Abrams Artists Agency, 275 Seventh Avenue, 26th Floor, New York, NY 10001.

M. BUTTERFLY Copyright 1986; 1988 by David Henry Hwang. Reprinted by Permission of David Henry Hwang. Contact: Writers and Artists Agency, 19 W. 44th Street, #1410, New York, NY 10036, (212) 391-1112.

THE MARRIAGE OF FIGARO Copyright 1991 translated by Richard Nelson. Reprinted by Permission of Peter Franklin a/a/f Richard Nelson. Contact: Broadway Play Publishing, (212) 627-1055.

MY CHILDREN, MY AFRICA Copyright 1989 by Athol Fugard. Reprinted by Permission of William Morris Agency, Inc. on behalf of the Author. CAUTION: Professionals and amateurs are hereby warned that "MY CHILDREN, MY AFRICA" is subject to a royalty. It is fully protected under the copyright laws of the United States of America, and of all countries covered by the International Copyright Union (including the Dominion of Canada and the rest of the British Commonwealth), and of all countries covered by the Pan-American Copyright Convention and the Universal Copyright Convention, the Berne Convention and of all countries with which the United States has reciprocal copyright relations. All rights, including professional/amateur stage rights, motion picture, recitation, lecturing, public reading, radio broadcasting, television, video or sound recording and all other forms of mechanical or electronic reproduction, such as CD-ROM, CD-I, information storage and retrieval systems and photocopying, and the rights of translation into foreign languages, are strictly reserved. Particular emphasis is placed upon the matter of readings, permission for which must be secured from the Author's agent in writing. Inquiries concerning rights should be addressed to William Morris Agency, Inc., 1325 Avenue of the Americas, New York, NY 10019, attn: Samuel Liff.

THE OWL AND THE PUSSYCAT Copyright 1965, 1993 by Bill Manhoff. Reprinted by permission of ICM (see Talley and Son for complete statement).

PEER GYNT Copyright 1979, 1951 translated by Paul Green. Reprinted by Permission of Samuel French, Inc. CAUTION: Professionals and amateurs are hereby warned that "PEER GYNT," being fully protected under the copyright laws of the United States of America, the British Commonwealth countries, including Canada, and the other countries of the Copyright Union, is subject to a royalty. All rights, including professional, amateur, motion picture, recitation, public reading, radio, television and cable broadcasting, and the rights of translation into foreign languages, are strictly reserved. Any inquiry regarding the availability of performance rights, or the purchase of individual copies of the authorized acting edition, must be directed to Samuel French Inc., 45 West 25th Street, New York, NY 10010, with other locations in Hollywood and Toronto, Canada.

PTERODACTYLS Copyright 1994, 1996 by Nicky Silver. Reprinted by Permission of Theatre Communications Group. Contact: TCG, 520 Eighth Avenue, 24th Floor, New York, NY 10018-4156.

RAISED IN CAPTIVITY Copyright 1995 by Nicky Silver. Reprinted by Permission of Theatre Communications Group. Contact: TCG, 520 Eighth Avenue, 24th Floor, New York, NY 10018-4156.

REMEMBER THIS Copyright 1999 by Stephen Poliakoff. Reprinted by permission of Methuen Drama. Contact: Judy Daish Associates, Ltd., 2 St. Charles Place, London W10 6EG, England.

SEA MARKS Copyright 1982 by Gardner McKay. Reprinted by Permission of the Author. Contact: Gardner McKay, (808) 395-8785.

THE SEAGULL Copyright 1994 translated by Carol Rocamora. Reprinted by Permission of the Author. Contact: Smith and Kraus Publishers, P.O. Box 127, Lyme, NH 03768.

SEVEN YEAR ITCH Copyright 1953, 1956, 1979, 1980 by George Axelrod. Reprinted by Permission of Dramatists Play Service. CAUTION: The excerpts from SEVEN YEAR ITCH included in this volume are reprinted by permission of Dramatists Play Service, Inc. The nonprofessional stage performance rights in this Play are controlled exclusively by Dramatists Play Service, Inc. No nonprofessional performance of the Play may be given without obtaining, in advance, the written permission of Dramatists Play Service, Inc., and paying the requisite fee. Inquiries concerning all other rights should be addressed to Dramatists Play Service, Inc., 440 Park Avenue South, New York, NY 10016.

SHADOWLANDS Copyright 1989 by William Nicholson. Reprinted by Permission of David Higham Associates Limited. Contact: David Higham Associates Limited, 5-8 Lower John Street, Golden Square, London WIF 9HA.

SHYSTER Copyright 2000 by Brian Goluboff. Reprinted by Permission of William Morris Agency, Inc. on behalf of the Author. CAUTION: Professionals and amateurs are hereby warned that "SHYSTER" is subject to a royalty. It is fully protected under the copyright laws of the United States of America, and of all countries covered by the International Copyright Union (including the Dominion of Canada and the rest of the British Commonwealth), and of all countries covered by the Pan-American Copyright Convention and the Universal Copyright Convention, the Berne Convention and of all countries with which the United States has reciprocal copyright relations. All rights, including professional/ amateur stage rights, motion picture, recitation, lecturing, public reading, radio broadcasting, television, video or sound recording and all other forms of mechanical or electronic reproduction, such as CD-ROM, CD-I, information storage and retrieval systems and photocopying, and the rights of translation into foreign languages, are strictly reserved. Particular emphasis is placed upon the matter of readings, permission for which must be secured from the Author's agent in writing. Inquiries concerning rights should be addressed to William Morris Agency, Inc., 1325 Avenue of the Americas, New York, NY 10019, attn: Jeremy Katz.

SIDE MAN Copyright 1998 by Swuigluie Productions, Inc. Reprinted by Permission of Grove/Atlantic, Inc. Contact: William Morris Agency, 1325 Avenue of the Americas, New York, NY 10019.

SIX DEGREES OF SEPARATION Copyright 1990 by John Guare. Reprinted by Permission of Author. Contact: Andrew Boose, 1 Dag Hammarskjold Plaza, New York, NY 10017.

SNAKEBIT Copyright 2000 by David Marshall Grant. Reprinted by Permission of Author. Contact: Creative Artists Agency, 767 Fifth Avenue, 10th Floor, New York, NY 10153.

SOPHISTRY Copyright1995 by Jonathan Marc Sherman. Reprinted by Permission of the Author. Contact: William Morris Agency, 1325 Avenue of the Americas, New York, NY 10019.

A STATE AFFAIR Copyright 2000 by Robin Soans. Reprinted by Permission of the author's agent. Contact: Kerry Gardner Management, 7 St. George's Square, London SW1V 2HX.

TALLEY AND SON Copyright 1986, 1995 by Lanford Wilson. Reprinted by Permission of International Creative Management, Inc. Contact: International Creative Management, 40 West 57th, New York, NY 10019.

THREE DAYS OF RAIN Copyright 1997 by Richard Greenberg. Reprinted by permission of Grove/Atlantic, Inc. Contact: William Morris Agency, 1325 Avenue of the Americas, New York, NY 10019.

TORCH SONG TRILOGY Copyright 1978, 1979 by Harvey Fierstein. Reprinted by Permission of Random House. Contact: Random House, Permissions Department, 1745 Broadway, New York, NY 10019.

TRIUMPH OF LOVE Copyright 1999 translated by Stephen Wadsworth. Reprinted by Permission of the Author. Contact: Smith and Kraus Publishers, P.O. Box 127, Lyme, NH 03768.

TRUST Copyright 1995 by Steven John Dietz. Reprinted by Permission of Author. CAUTION: The Stock and amateur rights are controlled exclusively by the Dramatists Play Service, Inc., 440 Park Avenue South, New York, NY 10016. No Stock or amateur performance of the play may be given without obtaining in advance the written permission of Dramatists Play Service Inc. and paying the requisite fee. For all other inquiries, contact: Sarah Jane Leigh, ICM, 40 W. 57th St., New York, NY 10019.

VISITING MR. GREEN Copyright 1999, 1994 by Jeff Baron. Reprinted by Permission of the Author. Reprinted by Permission of Mary Harden a/a/f the Author. CAUTION: Professionals and amateurs are hereby warned that performance of VISITING MR. GREEN is subject to a royalty. It is fully protected under the copyright laws of the United States of America, and of all countries covered by the International Copyright Union (including the Dominion of Canada and the rest of the British Commonwealth),